Older Couples:
New Romances

Older Couples: New Romances

FINDING & KEEPING LOVE IN LATER LIFE

Edith Ankersmit Kemp, L.C.S.W.
& Jerrold E. Kemp, Ed.D.

CELESTIAL ARTS
Berkeley, Toronto

Celestial Arts Publishing
P.O. Box 7123
Berkeley, California 94707
www.tenspeed.com

Celestial Arts titles are distributed in Canada by Ten Speed Canada,
in the United Kingdom and Europe by Airlift Books, in South Africa
by Real Books, in Australia by Simon & Schuster Australia, in New
Zealand by Southern Publishers Group, and in Southeast Asia by
Berkeley Books.

Cover and text design by Greene Design

Library of Congress Cataloging-in-Publication data available
from the publisher.

The first edition of this book with the title OLDER COUPLES: NEW
COUPLINGS was publsihed in 2001 by Unlimted Publishing, LLC

First printing 2002
Printed in the United States of America

1 2 3 4 5 6 / 06 05 04 03 02

According to the Lummis Indians of the Pacific Northwest, old age was the proper time to fall in love. Old age was the proper time to suffer romances, and jealousy, and lose your head—old age, when you felt things more, and could spare the time to go dead nuts over a person, and understand how fine a thing it was. This is how the Lummis saw it.

Annie Dillard, *The Living*. New York, HarperCollins, 1992.

Endorsements

This visionary book is replete with experienced guides to the deeply personal territory of second-chance relationships in later years. The stories and information map the opportunities and pitfalls of such liaisons for later-life renewal of joy and love.

Jay Thorwaldson, editor

Palo Alto (California) Weekly

Older Couples: New Romances is a welcome resource for older adults who are in, or thinking about, forming new relationships. Based on extensive interviews, it offers interesting and helpful insights into the complex process of finding and nurturing new partnerships. Demonstrating that it's never too late, this book provides a unique look at the ageless wonder of becoming a couple again.

Barrie Robinson, MSW

Gerontology Lecturer, School of Social Welfare, University of California, Berkeley

A fascinating book, depicting the many different types of newly-formed love relationships experienced by elders. This is an excellent resource, not only for older folks and their concerned children but for classes studying the sociology of aging.

Dr. Glen Caspers Doyle, Professor

Interdisciplinary Gerontology Program, College of Health and Human Services, California State University, Fresno

This book provides older persons a resource of how to navigate the uncertain waters of new loves in later life and it gives voice to issues of romance and intimacy rarely articulated in academic gerontology courses.

Dr. Brian de Vries, Professor and Director

Gerontology Programs, San Francisco State University

Comments from Our Readers

We're happily married and can identify with many of the couples described in this book. It reaffirms and reinforces the enjoyable way we conduct our life together. Every older couple should read it ... they can learn from it.

AE, Walnut Creek, California

My husband and I, in our sixties, have been together for six months. We have many arguments and differences. Your book has enabled us to better understand each other and work things out. The experiences of many couples, along with useful suggestions, make this a valuable reading.

DW, Oakhurst, California

My dad died two years ago and my mother has been lonely ever since. When I showed her your book, she became interested in finding a new relationship. Tonight she has her third date! The section on *How Do You Find a Partner?* was particularly helpful to her.

RF, Sacramento, California

You say your book is for older couples. I am 41 and my new husband is 44. Boy, has your book been helpful to us! It should be read by any couple starting a second relationship.

SZ, Monterey, California

Contents

Acknowledgements

Thanks to Judith Wallerstein whose book *The Good Marriage* gave us the inspiration for this project. Acknowledgement to James Landers for his literature search that found no book dealing with relationships formed in later life. Our gratitude to Rachel Oliver, psychologist, who interviewed us so that we could experience the process before Edith interviewed others. We owe our greatest debt to the couples who so freely shared their joys and struggles. Their motivation was the desire to help others in similar situations.

We wish to recognize our professional colleagues who reviewed our book, many of whom provided helpful suggestions. They include Midge Wood, Pat Spohn, Blanche Jaggi, Jaqueline Ensign, Vera Lis, Jane Loebel, Barbara Leff, Jay Thorwaldson, Barrie Robinson, Glen Doyle, Brian de Vries and Judith Wallerstein.

Thanks to Kristina Rylands for her assistance with the first edition in editing and in choosing themes for the interview chapters; estate attorney Lynn Rice, who consulted with us to ensure the accuracy of the chapter dealing with legal matters; and Denise Metzger who handled the final editing and formatting of the first manuscript. Finally, our appreciation to Veronica Randall for her thoughtful and effective efforts in editing this manuscript.

Preface

EDITH

 We were introduced to each other by mutual friends. Jerry was 75. His wife had died a year and a half earlier. I was 66 and had been a widow for four years. No more than a month passed before we knew we loved each other and, living a three-hour drive apart, we visited as often as we could.

Nine months after we met, I moved from my urban home to Jerry's country house. I brought some of my furniture and changed almost everything on the walls. The house was dark, so we installed skylights. Jerry knew I wanted as much as possible to make it our home, and he went along with my changes. But the decorations he likes best are the ones we bought together.

JERRY

 During that first year of living together, we enjoyed sharing activities such as hiking, square dancing, watching public television programs together, and visiting each other's friends. Our life was full of fun, joy, passion (yes, at our ages!), and a lot of adjustments. Habits formed over many years of living without each other caused the most conflicts. Edith forgot to turn off lights and close the toilet seat cover, both of which bugged me to no end. I am extremely punctual, and we had some blow-ups about Edith keeping me waiting. When she first moved in, every table surface was covered with papers, journals, and books. Dust and cobwebs were everywhere. Edith has since learned to be more punctual, and now I strive to keep the house clean and orderly, except for my desk, which we have agreed can stay a mess. Edith still forgets a light sometimes, but I just turn it off. Some things still bother me, but I keep my mouth shut. (Edith hates being lectured to and I know it.)

One year after we moved in together, we married. Though we are still making adjustments, and will be doing so for the rest of our lives, our time together is much smoother. We began to wonder how other older couples forming new relationships made their adjustments. What habits did they change? How did they learn to accept, or at least tolerate, each other's behaviors? What about finances, health, sexuality, hobbies, eating habits, entertainment, and relationships with children and grandchildren?

EDITH

 These questions piqued our curiosity. I am a licensed psychotherapist, and have worked with couples for many years, examining the patterns in their relationships and finding ways to improve their interactions. Jerry is the author of three textbooks in his field and has brought his considerable writing and organizational skills to this book. As partners in a newly formed older-couple relationship, we wanted to discover how other older couples thought, dealt with their problems, and made their decisions. Our plan was to offer those who were either involved in an older-couple relationship or contemplating one, the opportunity to learn from others in similar situations. We also hoped to offer practical advice and suggestions that our readers could apply to their own lives.

Our inspiration came from Judith Wallerstein's thoughtful book, *The Good Marriage*. Of the many couples she interviewed, the only older pair had been together since their early twenties. We searched and found little written about older couples forming new relationships.

We know that people are now living longer, leading to the potential for more and more older individuals to form new relationships. This conclusion is supported by statistics from the 2000 Census:

- From 1980 to 2000, the number of persons 65 years of age and older in the United States increased by nine million.

- From 1980 to 2000, the number of widowed and divorced seniors increased by 16.6%.

- The number of women over the age of 60 who married doubled between 1990 and 2000.

Here are two statements resulting from a survey in 2000 by the National Council on Aging:

- Americans are moving toward a new old age…an age in which people add life to their years as well as years to their lives.

- Vital aging is attainable for most Americans. The latter third of our life can be either our highlight years or twilight years: more of a choice for personal fulfillment rather than a matter of luck or genes.

Today's senior citizens are healthier, more active, and receive better medical attention than ever before. Therefore, older people may be more likely to want to form new relationships, enjoying their remaining years in pleasurable sharing with others.

As we prepared to locate potential couples to interview, we recognized the different arrangements that people make today in their personal lives. Therefore, we sought couples either married, living together, or living separately but in a committed relationship. We required at least one partner to be over age 55 when their relationship began and that they had been together for at least a year so there would be time to experience problems and make adjustments. We included a number of couples who had been together for many years. This allowed us to examine the changes taking place within relatively new relationships, as well as over time and with increasing age.

To attract couples for the book, we publicized our project in urban, suburban, and rural areas of Northern California. Based on her more than twenty-five years of experience as a counselor, Edith conducted the interviews.

This is an anecdotal rather than a statistical study. We do not claim to measure the success or failure of late-life marriages in any particular population. Our sample is small and self-selected. Most of our couples were delighted with their relationships and wanted to share their stories. (Naturally, they all experienced some problems and had adjustments to make.) We attempted to interest minority couples in our study; unfortunately, with no success. We do, however, cover a wide range of socio-economic levels, ages, educational and cultural backgrounds, and approaches to life. We hope that you will find their stories interesting and encouraging, and their experiences useful in your own life.

For the interviews, a range of questions was developed, including: *How did you meet? What attracted you to each other? How did your relationship develop? What kinds of problems did you face and what adjustments did you make?* Each person provided information about his or her family history, previous relationships, religious practices, financial arrangements, health, and sexuality.

Generally, there were three interview sessions. Usually Edith visited with each partner individually in the couple's home or in their separate homes. She then interviewed the two jointly. Occasionally, when appropriate, she only met with a couple together. A complete interview lasted from three to five hours and was recorded on tape. Every effort was made to keep the identities of our couples confidential without losing the nature of their personalities or the flavor of the relationships. We very much appreciate the openness of those who cooperated and believe the experience was enjoyable and often beneficial to the participants.

Interspersed throughout the interviews are Edith's observations, which highlight important principles or practices. They are based on her knowledge as a psychotherapist and her personal experience as a widow who has formed a fulfilling new relationship.

Sometimes the topics discussed during the individual meetings revealed differences that were reviewed in the third session. Some couples used this joint session to better understand their differences, and to better appreciate the good relations they had established between themselves. One pair said, "This interview is reminding us of how much we love each other."

We came to this study with a mindset that older couples might encounter serious adjustment difficulties. To our surprise, we found a great deal more positive than negative responses. Many interviewees reported that they have more joy, more freedom, greater affection, and better sex than they found in their earlier relationships. This was true for those who were widowed as well as for those who had been divorced. We wondered why and discovered a number of possible reasons for these enriched late-in-life relationships. For example, age comes with experiences, many of them painful. They can result in greater maturity, patience, and appreciation for the essentials in life, including the knowledge that our time is limited. Also, there are no longer children to raise, and with most individuals, no jobs to go to with demanding schedules and responsibilities. This allows more time and energy for new partners to enjoy each other. To avoid the irritability that can result from too much togetherness, we found that most of our interviewees arranged for some degree of separateness. This varies from living apart to finding private places in the same house, or engaging in individual activities from time to time.

Following are a few principles that the couples interviewed have taught us.

- Later in life an individual's beliefs, lifestyle, and habits are more set. Some adjustments can be made, but the primary key to a good relationship is acceptance of your partner as he or she is.

- Sexual satisfaction is possible throughout life. Age is no barrier.

- Adult children may or may not be pleased with the new relationship. If, unfortunately, they are not, it is important to keep your commitment to each other primary.

- Financial arrangements need to be discussed early in your relationship, with particular attention given to how expenses will be shared.

- Be aware that as your partner ages, you may become a caretaker. It is normal to have some feelings of resentment. As long as your actions express care and affection, you need not blame yourself for your feelings.

Whether you are an older person contemplating a new relationship or you are in a relationship that is having difficulties, we hope this book can provide some insights and suggestions. We owe a great deal to those who so freely shared their intimate thoughts, feelings, joys, and struggles in the hopes that they could be helpful to other older folks embarking on new love and a new life together.

Edith Ankersmit Kemp and Jerrold E. Kemp

PART ONE:

Introducing Our Couples

CHAPTER 1

Life Is Short:
Eat Dessert First

Joanne and Andy

He's an intellectual. She's a woman with a showgirl personality. She likes rock music; he's into classical. They're attractive, intelligent, and deeply in love. Both have been divorced and have gone through hard times. In their new relationship, they are learning to compromise and share while each maintains a distinct individuality.

Balancing Separateness and Togetherness

Joanne and Andy illustrate a universal theme in all relationships—maintaining a balance between separateness and togetherness. This is especially important with couples who have spent many years living separate lives with different habits, preferences, and interests. Joanne and Andy are most articulate about this theme. They demonstrate that individuals *can* grow throughout life and that pain from the past can help us treasure the present.

Introducing Joanne and Andy

Joanne is 59 and Andy is 60. They rent an apartment in the center of a busy city with high-rise buildings, shopping centers, and congested traffic. They had begun dating 14 months earlier and had been living together for eight months. When I arrived, Andy was out on an errand. Joanne graciously ushered me into their spacious and elegantly furnished apartment.

Joanne looked much younger than her years. She had stylishly cut black hair and was very attractive, outgoing, and articulate. Andy, who arrived later, was a husky, balding man with warm, brown eyes. He was slower to warm up than Joanne, but he gradually relaxed, became more candid and forthcoming. He had a sparkle in his eyes and an engaging smile.

How Did You Meet?

Joanne was vice president in charge of marketing for a large corporation. One afternoon she was walking through her building and approached a company accountant she knew only on a casual basis. He was standing with another colleague talking about jazz. As Joanne passed, she flippantly said "93.6" (the FM frequency for the local jazz station). This remark caught Andy's attention.

A few days later when Joanne saw Andy in the lunchroom, she sneezed, and he reacted with, "Bless you, my child." "Thank you, Father," Joanne replied. He asked, "Are you of that ilk?" "I was," she responded. Andy invited Joanne to his office for a chat and they discovered each had been raised Catholic. This was followed by an invitation to a jazz concert, and so they began dating.

How Were You Attracted to Each Other?

When Andy first noticed Joanne, he was captivated by her lively walk, which showed a jaunty spirit. Immediately interested, he looked her up in the company's employee database, finding her age and marital status.

What had attracted Joanne? "Trust was a big issue with me, and I trusted Andy almost from the beginning. He's the first man I've wanted to hold hands with while walking down the street. I feel at peace with him."

How Did Your Relationship Develop?

Joanne and Andy began living together when she left the company to start her own consulting business and he retired. They moved to a large apartment where each could have their own separate room. They also had individual phone numbers and post office boxes. Most of the furniture was Joanne's. She told me, "Andy didn't have a home—he had a place to live. It looked like a motel room." The home they shared had tasteful décor and was meticulously neat, except for Andy's room.

What Were Your Early Lives Like?

Joanne and Andy had remarkably similar childhood backgrounds. They both came from working-class Catholic families. Joanne's parents fought frequently, and her father was a volatile alcoholic and a gambler. She was the eldest child and described herself as the family peacemaker.

Andy was the second of seven children in a poor immigrant family. His father was a stern disciplinarian who frequently beat the four boys. Joanne and Andy believed that their similar upbringings helped bind them together.

What Were Your Previous Relationships Like?

Andy

Andy had a previous marriage that lasted 21 years, with a decade of sullen noncommunication and no sex. He was never unfaithful and waited until their daughter was 18 before he left his wife.

EDITH

 This demonstrates Andy's basic integrity, trustworthiness, and sense of responsibility. Joanne had enough life experience to know that trust is one of the most important features of any relationship. Young people often are drawn together by physical features, while many older couples recognize that trust and integrity are more important.

I also see integrity as a key factor. If the basic love, care, and sense of responsibility exist between two people, I have hope that, with help, differences can be resolved. Joanne, sensing Andy's trustworthiness, was willing to ride out the many small disagreements between them.

My husband Jerry had a companionable marriage, although his wife, because of emotional difficulties and a long illness, had little interest in sex. He faithfully remained with her for 45 years until her death. This was an indication to me of those same qualities in Jerry that Joanne saw in Andy.

After their divorce, Andy was single for nine years, during which time he was very active sexually. (Says Joanne on the side, "Like a rabbit!")

Joanne

Joanne was married for 23 years to her first husband with whom she had two daughters. They had known each other since she was 18. Joanne described the marriage as loveless, not much affection, not good sex. A homemaker for many years, she went back to school at age 35 for her college degree. Ultimately, it was she who left the marriage.

Joanne was with her second husband for nine difficult years. He was manic–depressive, had a violent temper, was verbally abusive, and, on several occasions, struck her in anger. One day, she went into the garage and found him dead, his body hanging from the vacuum cleaner cord. This tragedy, along with other losses, including deaths in her family and children moving away, left her with "a hole in my heart as big as a Mack truck" and understandably skittish about forming a new relationship.

Joanne eventually became involved with a wealthy man who was 20 years her senior and who had recently lost his wife. She described their four–year relationship as a mutually supportive friendship with occasional sex. She was still seeing him when she met Andy, and their parting was friendly.

EDITH

 Earlier we learned that Joanne was the eldest child and the family "peacemaker." When a child in this position becomes an adult, he or she often assumes a caretaker role in relationships. Joanne certainly did this with her second husband, but as much as she tried, she could not help him. Naturally she was cautious about forming a new relationship. Her union with an older man was not a deep involvement but was very much a safe haven after the intensity of her second marriage. Because she was not deeply in love, she felt safe and was able to recover from the pain of her husband's suicide. It gave her time to be ready to love Andy.

How Do You Balance Interests, Habits, and Activities?

Joanne and Andy saw themselves as "two circles coming together but still trying to keep our own identities." The way they balanced their activities, allowing for both separate and quality together times, concretely shows how the two circles can come together, while allowing them to keep their unique, individual qualities intact.

Joanne liked almost any movie, while Andy preferred intellectual and foreign films. Sometimes they went to the movies together, sometimes separately. Joanne enjoyed a type of rock music that Andy didn't care for, while he preferred listening to classical selections. Other than good jazz, which they both liked, they tolerated each other's music. They had three television sets in the apartment for *his, hers*, and *our* programs. They ate together whenever possible and both were vegetarians before they met. They enjoyed taking short walks, bicycling, and going to jazz concerts together.

Both Joanne and Andy had to change several of their own habits while accepting some of their partner's. Andy was used to dropping his things on the floor, picking them up only for guests, and leaving the dishes in the sink until it was full. The first adjustment he made when they began to live together was with neatness. "I just did it," said Andy with pride. The day I visited, Joanne was about to leave for a two-week visit with her daughter. Andy knew the apartment would become a mess while she was gone, but he would straighten it up before she returned. He lets things go when he is alone, but he knows that Joanne wants a neat home and makes a real effort to please her.

Joanne also has habits that bother Andy. She often forgets to close the refrigerator. She sets her purse on the kitchen counter, although Andy is concerned it might have been on a dirty floor. Wisely, he doesn't make an issue of it.

Andy has a room of his own in their apartment where he keeps his clothes and other personal items. They sleep together in the master bedroom, but the closets in that room are for Joanne's use. They have separate bathrooms and Joanne laughed,

"I think sharing a bathroom would have done in our relationship."

EDITH

I like Joanne's humor. It is a saving factor in any relationship. It helps to laugh at ourselves. Jerry and I keep a spark lit between us with humor, thus greatly diffusing any conflict.

The issue of keeping his own identity is especially important to Andy. He explains, "One change that is happening because of our relationship is that lots of the things that were important to me in the past I have given up. I wonder if it's going to haunt me someday. I don't know. The whole cycle of a relationship starts out with two people knocking themselves out to please one another. Then they gradually attempt to find what they want and take tentative steps to get it. That's about where I am now."

EDITH

Here Andy is particularly articulate about finding the right balance between accommodating each other and holding on to what is especially important to each individual. In tolerating each other's music when together, Joanne and Andy accommodate each other. By having their own television sets, they respect their different preferences and hold on to a sense of individual autonomy. In a happy relationship, partners both give up a little to please each other and maintain the basic tastes and values that are essential parts of themselves.

It is important to consider the following issues when balancing autonomy and togetherness:

• What can you do together?

- What can you, without resentment, allow your partner to enjoy separately?

- What habits can you change?

- What can you accept in your partner?

Resolving these small issues is a good part of what makes a successful relationship.

What Makes This Relationship Work So Well?

When I saw Joanne and Andy together, the sparkle, humor, and affection between them were obvious. At one point Andy looked at Joanne and said "You're everything I ever wanted. I'm not settling for less at all." Joanne laughed and blushed, saying, "How can I resist him?"

Then Andy explained with sincerity, "In Joanne I seem to have found most of the things I value in a person. She's attractive, sexual, bright, and competent. She doesn't take any crap from me, which I admire a lot. I can be a bully like my father. This woman can't be frightened. Our relationship is much more important than any disagreements we might have."

"I realize that we don't have forever in terms of time," Joanne continued. "We're not going to raise children together. I've been through menopause. We've come to a different place in our lives. It's wonderful to find a companion. See that little plaque up on the wall? *'Life's Uncertain, Eat Dessert First.'* I think we both have had life experiences that have made us realize what's really important. Andy is a cancer survivor and went through a very tragic period in his life. My second husband committed suicide at a time when everyone who was important to me left. When you experience so much sadness, I think you look at life differently. You hunger for joy because life is so very uncertain. When you go through such traumas and survive, you're never quite the same. What might have been important then isn't important now. What I might have said before, I don't say today. If I could go back and relive my first marriage with the knowledge and experience I now have, I think even that might have succeeded."

As they were still in a relatively early stage of their relationship, Joanne and Andy had concerns about long-term commitment and different perspectives. Joanne spoke frankly: "Andy talks about being together forever. I've had too many losses and unpleasant situations. I just want to live for now." She was afraid of the possessiveness and control that she saw as an inevitable part of a marriage. She worried that her spending habits, especially on clothes, would become a source of tension. When asked if he would be upset if she spent $2,000 on her wardrobe, Andy said that, frankly, he would be annoyed.

Andy underscored his long-term commitment: "Recently, on the way to visit my mother, I knew Joanne was the most important person in my life and would remain so." On the other hand, Joanne believes, "We could be talking of living together for two years or for twenty years." They both talk about a long-term relationship, but are a little gun–shy. They use phrases such as: "We're going to make it through the day." "It's a-day-to-day thing." "We're still in the stage where we're hoping."

I said goodbye to Joanne and Andy as Joanne dashed off to a hair appointment, in preparation for a two–week visit with her daughter.

Some Final Thoughts

This couple offers an excellent example of how to balance separateness and togetherness. By successfully doing this early in their relationship, I believe they are on their way to a long and happy union.

Joanne and Andy also illustrate how a difficult childhood can lead to painful marriage experiences. Certainly Joanne's did. She chose a volatile, unstable, but perhaps exciting second husband, much like her father. I would presume that Andy stopped himself from being expressive and seeking affection because of his upbringing in a large family with a stern, physically abusive father. Thus he endured a lengthy, cold and distant marriage. But Joanne and Andy also are a shining example of how, by learning from the past, old patterns can be overcome. It is never too late to experience the sharing, love, and affection for which humans deeply long.

With the loss of our spouses and then of dear friends, Jerry and I have gained a deeper appreciation of living in the present ... a thankfulness for each moment of each day. Today, we are keenly aware that our time is limited. We both have had, as did Joanne and Andy, much sadness in our lives. Therefore, every day of our new life together is a gift to savor. We do "eat dessert first."

CHAPTER 2

A Second Life with a New Love

Ruth and Paul

After her first husband died, Ruth made up her mind not to get married again. Then a friend from long ago, whose first wife was entirely incapacitated with Alzheimer's disease, invited her to attend a conference with him. He mailed her an airline ticket, and enclosed a brochure from the hotel showing a picture of a guest room with a king-size bed. "What a presumptuous rascal," she thought. And so began a meaningful relationship leading to a happy marriage.

Renewing Life's Joy after Years of Caretaking

Caring for a seriously ill loved one over many years is so all-consuming that one can lose part of oneself. What a delight it must be to find yourself again with a new love. Life did go on for Ruth and Paul, and continues to do so.

Introducing Ruth and Paul

It was a long, trying 20 miles on the dusty dirt road to their home, and the drive seemed to take forever. The few visible house numbers were confusing, and I thought I might be lost. I pulled up to a dilapidated old trailer and was told that Ruth and Paul lived just down the road. Sure enough, I climbed a hill and found, to my surprise after all the heat and dust, a large redwood house surrounded by flower and vegetable gardens and a barn with a corral for animals. Both Ruth and Paul came to the door to greet me. Ruth is a tall slender woman with short gray hair and blue eyes sparkling in her pleasantly wrinkled face. Paul is a handsome man of medium build, slightly heavy, with a warm smile. Both were dressed in carefully pressed pants and shirts. We made ourselves comfortable around the kitchen table, and our interview began.

Ruth is 78 years old and Paul is 80. They have been married seven years, and both had been widowed. They live on a ranch that originally belonged to Ruth and her first husband. After our interview, I got a tour of the house and grounds. Their home is spacious and comfortable. The furnishings are of oriental design, and I was interested to see a striking silk tapestry of a Japanese ceremony. When they decided that Paul would move in, they had the bedroom enlarged, and a new bathroom and a large closet were added for Paul.

How Did You Meet?

During World War II, Paul, Ruth, and Ruth's first husband all worked for the same defense contractor. Ruth was in a clerical position, her husband was a machinist, and Paul, who was also married, was in quality control. The two couples met at a social gathering, and their friendship began. They often had dinner together and enjoyed each other's company.

Then Paul entered military service, while Ruth and her husband continued their employment with the defense contractor. The two couples kept in contact, particularly through the exchange of annual Christmas cards and letters. In 1970, Paul, who owned a building-supply company at the time, provided Ruth and her husband with materials to renovate their newly purchased ranch.

Eleven years later, Ruth's husband passed away. She mentioned this in her Christmas card to Paul and his wife. Some years later, a Christmas letter from Paul informed Ruth that his wife was suffering from Alzheimer's. Not knowing the extent of his wife's illness, Ruth sent him an article about the reputed benefits of blue algae in alleviating Alzheimer's symptoms. When Paul phoned to thank her, she invited him to her ranch, more than 200 miles from his home.

"Would it really be all right?" asked Paul, ever considerate. "What will the neighbors think?"

"I don't have any neighbors," laughed Ruth, knowing how isolated her property was.

So Paul accepted her invitation. Although they hadn't seen each other for 17 years, their friendship was easily renewed, and they had a delightful, very proper visit. Paul really enjoyed Ruth's pot roast and apple pie. "She's a wonderful cook," he told me.

How Were You Attracted to Each Other?

Ruth recalled her impression of Paul when, many years earlier, he stopped by her office at work. He was cheerful and radiant, with a twinkle in his eye, and a charming sense of humor. "If someone in the office went to help Paul before I could, I was disappointed." Thus, she liked him from the start.

Paul also remembered Ruth from those days. "She was vivacious and pleasant to work with; a genuine, outgoing personality."

Both Ruth and Paul were, and still are, confident, extroverted personalities, and they acknowledge and appreciate these traits in each other. Though their lives went in different directions for many years, their mutual attraction remained, leading to the thought that both of them expressed: "It was nice to renew our friendship again."

How Did Your Relationship Develop?

Paul was happy and excited about reconnecting with Ruth. However, he thought he should not contact her right away because, "she'd think I was too anxious." About a month later he phoned her, and again the next month. At this stage they were just "friendship" calls. Ruth enjoyed talking with Paul but, although she liked him a lot, she had made up her mind she would *not* marry again.

Paul had been taking care of his ailing wife for ten years, and he had had little, if any, real companionship. As he said, "When I saw Ruth so full of life and energy, I realized how nice it would be to have that kind of partnership again."

Paul had sold his building-supply company and became director of sales for a larger, similar company. His new position included lots of traveling around the country, with local hotels providing complimentary rooms and meals. An opportunity for such a trip became available, and he asked Ruth to accompany him. At first, she was uncertain about joining him, but she had friends in the city to which they would travel, and she could stay with them. So she accepted Paul's invitation and told him she would make her own arrangements. Then she received the ticket and the brochure with the king–size bed.

After having second thoughts, Ruth said to herself: "I'm 71 and he's 73 years old. Why should I be such a prude?" She went and had a wonderful time. Oh yes, she also visited her friends but stayed in the hotel with Paul and became sexually involved with him. A photo taken during that first trip together shows the two of them looking glowing and jubilant.

In the months that followed, they visited frequently, meeting at each other's homes. After considering their children's feelings and their own religious ethics, they agreed not to live together without marrying. Because Paul's wife was still alive, it was necessary for him to obtain a divorce, with the stipulation that he would continue to financially support his debilitated wife until her death. (This is not an infrequent practice in such situations.) He did so until she died, six years after he and Ruth were married.

After the divorce was official, they were married at the church in Ruth's rural community, followed by a reception at her home. Their children and 150 friends came, happily accepting this new relationship. Paul and Ruth honeymooned in Bermuda. As they talked about their happy memories of the wedding, a sweet glow animated their faces.

For the first five years of their marriage, they maintained Paul's house for monthly visits to his first wife's nursing home. Over time, the costs of maintaining his separate home began to escalate, so Paul decided to sell. His children took over the task of regular visits with their mother, even though she no longer recognized them. After a five-year transition period, Paul found that he could close out the 42 years of his previous life and not miss it. He had made a new life with Ruth.

What Were Your Previous Relationships Like?

Ruth

Ruth was married at age 18 and had one daughter. It was a good and loving marriage. After two decades years together, her husband contracted emphysema and, for his health, they decided to leave the city to get out of the smog. They purchased their ranch in 1970, and her husband retired at age 57. For two years they worked at renovating the property and moved there in 1972. The cleaner air made Ruth's husband feel much better at first, but gradually his condition deteriorated. Within four years, his activities became increasingly limited. By 1978 he was bedridden. In addition to the emphysema, he had severe back problems and was hospitalized for three months after back surgery. He required strong pain medication and oxygen before he died in 1981 of congestive heart failure. Ruth and her husband knew he was dying. His protracted illness gave them time to cry together and time to say goodbye.

For five long years Ruth took care of everything, including nursing duties like bathing and administering medication. She took care of all the household chores plus all the work on the ranch. She tended the horses, cattle, ducks, and worked in the gardens. It was exhausting, and yet for Ruth, all these responsibilities helped her to keep her balance. One way she took care of herself was to take every Wednesday afternoon off to meet with a quilting group.

Understandably, her husband became more and more irritable as his health worsened. Ruth still regrets once saying, "If you were this crabby when we first knew each other, I never would have married you."

"Words are like bullets shot from a gun. Once they're out, you can't take them back," she told me with tears in her eyes.

EDITH

 I think Ruth was being hard on herself. Caring for a seriously ill loved one is extremely draining, both emotionally and physically, and it is very difficult to be continually patient with the patient!

After her husband's death, Ruth lived alone on the ranch for more than nine years. At first, the loss of her husband felt like a loss of part of herself. Gradually, her outlook began to change as she attended community meetings, saw her women friends, and gave dinner parties. "But," said Ruth, "Never in my wildest dreams did I expect to be as happy again as I am now in my new life with Paul. It is possible to love a second time."

EDITH

 I very much identify with Ruth, although my caretaking lasted only three months, while Ruth's went on for more than five years. Like Ruth's husband, my late husband became irritable when in pain, and there were times when I lost my temper. I regret those times, but I have forgiven myself, as I hope Ruth forgives herself. Also like Ruth and her first husband, my late husband and I had time to review our life together and to say goodbye. I was able to take off from work to be his primary caretaker. Hospice provided a part-time aide so that I could do the grocery shopping and even see a few clients. But despite the help, caring for my husband consumed me.

As Ruth held on to a part of herself by working on the ranch, my work as a psychotherapist was a saving grace. Certainly I never imagined then, nor in the years of grief after my husband's death, that I would one day find myself, as did Ruth, in a joyful life with a new love.

Paul

Paul had married at age 20, while still in college, and had three children with his first wife. Today, he enjoys his nine grandchildren and six great-grandchildren.

Paul was 62 when his wife first began to exhibit symptoms of Alzheimer's disease. "She often traveled with me when I was working. One evening she couldn't find our room in the hotel. Another time she couldn't find her way home from the local beauty shop. Soon I had to take her car keys away and drive her everywhere."

Paul hired a live-in maid who served as a caretaker while he was away at his job. His wife remained at home for nine years before he finally placed her in a long-term care facility. Her deterioration during these years was heart breaking. "I'd arrive home from work, and she'd look at me and say, 'When are you taking me home?' She didn't know who I was or who she was." Paul was visibly upset as he continued, "Life was closing in on me. I had only my work and my concern for my wife. I never knew from day to day what crisis would come next. She became belligerent and one time threw an iron at the maid, whom I had to take to the hospital for stitches."

Unfortunately, none of Paul's children lived nearby, so they had no opportunity to see the heavy toll their mother's disease was taking on their father. It wasn't until each child took her into their home for a short stay that they gained a better understanding of the difficulties he faced.

Paul went on, "My work and the traveling it entailed helped me to keep my sanity. It was an escape for me, and I still feel guilty about it."

EDITH

 My heart goes out to the families of those suffering from Alzheimer's disease. What a loss it is of the person they used to know and love. My mother had Alzheimer's, and before she died she didn't know who I was or even who she was. It brought home to me graphically how much our sense of identity is made up of memories. When we lose those memories, we lose the sense of who we are and who our dear ones are. Thus, Paul had already lost his wife long before he became involved with Ruth.

I know from personal experience that placing an

Alzheimer's patient in a nursing home does not remove the emotional burden. After my mother was admitted to an excellent facility where she received very good care, I had almost daily phone calls from the staff. She refused to take baths. She tried to run away. And so it went until her death.

Paul's conflicted feelings were perfectly understandable under such sadly trying circumstances. Just as Ruth was "saved" by her ranch, Paul's job kept his concern for his wife from consuming him completely.

Paul put his arm around Ruth and told me, "We hold on to fond memories of our departed mates. And we know we can always share these memories with each other."

Ruth responded, "We are both mature and have no jealousy about our past relationships."

Paul added, "That's true. And we thank God every day for the happiness we have found in our love for each other."

What Are Your Lives Like Today?

Ruth and Paul described very few problems in their relationship. (One adjustment that they did make is described in Chapter 21, *Monetary and Legal Arrangements*.) Certainly they represent a happy, well-adjusted older couple. They proudly displayed their collections of photographs from their travels in Australia, New Zealand, the Caribbean, Hong Kong, Thailand, and Europe. Said Paul, "We won't stop traveling until we have to."

EDITH

 They are fortunate. Not all older couples have the financial security or good enough health to travel so extensively.

They cooperate on many household chores. While Ruth does the cooking, Paul sets the table. He dries the dishes as Ruth washes. Paul helps Ruth with house cleaning, and they make their bed together. They enjoy sharing chores in their gardens and looking after their animals. Ruth wants Paul to look nice, so she spends time ironing his clothes, although he believes this is unnecessary. Paul likes to read mystery novels, and Ruth continues to meet with her quilting group each week.

As our discussion concluded, Ruth thoughtfully said, "At this point in life, we don't have to face the problems we had in our first marriages, when there were so many things that were new to us. Now we know what's required, and things go along more smoothly. Life is easier now and we have more fun."

Some Final Thoughts

Ruth and Paul are an example of two mature, loving individuals who devotedly cared for seriously ill spouses for many years. When a person is in the midst of such an experience, it can be all consuming with little left over for anyone or anything else. Ironically, other responsibilities, such as a job or a pet or a garden, often can be a godsend, as they offer ways by which one can hold on to an integral part of one's self.

Years, months, or even a few weeks of caretaking can provide the time to say goodbye to a loved one. During this process, it is very difficult to imagine that you will ever love again, or indeed, ever be truly happy again. But Ruth and Paul *did* find love and joy in their new life together, and their losses have made this happiness even more precious.

CHAPTER 3

Health Changes with Time, but Affection Lasts

Naomi and David

"There are days when I'm so sorry I got into this relationship, because I can't paint, I can't do this, I can't do that ... and there are other days when I say 'Thank god I've got him!'"

Entering the Caretaker Role

Although David is just three years older than Naomi, his health and memory have declined in the past few years. Naomi's straightforward, honest approach was instructive and enlightening. Her advice to women readers, based on her experience, is "If you marry an older man, you're going to be a nurse." But there is no lack of love in her honesty.

Introducing Naomi and David

Naomi was 64 when they met; David was 67. Now she's 78 and he's 81. Naomi had been widowed since she was 46, more than 18 years, when she met David, whose wife had died a few months earlier. With this couple, it is interesting to follow the changes over time; 14 years of togetherness, with 13 years of marriage.

David and Naomi live in a large retirement community. As I entered the apartment, the mezuzah on the door clearly identified their Judaism. Inside the sunny, spacious apartment were many paintings depicting Jewish life, including the Torah, the Sabbath candles, and a rabbi, all painted by Naomi. She is an intelligent, energetic woman who talks and laughs easily and is pleasant to look at. She is somewhat tall with short, curly gray hair. David is a friendly, cheerful man of medium height, slightly built, and neatly dressed in a tan shirt and matching tan slacks.

How Did You Meet?

They were living in the same city; David in his large family home, and Naomi in an apartment. She sold her house 12 years after her husband's death. One evening, Naomi's friend invited her to their synagogue to hear a woman rabbi preside, while David was there to say prayers for his recently deceased wife. When they met, he asked Naomi to go to dinner following the service. She declined, as she and her friend had planned to dine out together, but she gave him her phone number.

David called her later that night and was at her house by 9:00 the next morning! He wore shorts and, as Naomi said with a smile, "He looked adorable." They spent the whole day together, ate dinner out that night, and later danced in her apartment. They have seen each other every day ever since.

EDITH

 David certainly wasted no time in connecting with Naomi! I believe that for David, it was very difficult for him to be alone. Men tend not to have the same social and support circle as do women, and so often a man's wife is his only intimate friend. Little boys are usually socialized not to express feelings, so often it is difficult for men to allow themselves much time to grieve. Both of these factors will motivate a man to find a new partner fairly soon after a wife's death, sometimes to avoid loneliness and grief.

How Were You Attracted to Each Other?

After many years alone, Naomi was finally ready for an intimate relationship. "David was attractive and fun. I didn't want a great intellectual; I've had enough of that. He's very likable. He likes the whole world. I'm very, very happy. There are days I'd like to break his neck, but that has nothing to do with 'us'. He's very right for me at this stage of my life." I asked Naomi, why not at an earlier stage? "If we were raising children, he would love the kids to pieces but wouldn't push them enough intellectually." Finally, the fact that David was Jewish and involved in the temple were very important to her.

What attracted David to Naomi? He liked her hair, her body, the way she looked and dressed. "She was different, full of pep and smiles. I liked the way she moved her hands during that first service when I saw her. It was like leading an orchestra, and she still does it!"

How Did Your Relationship Develop?

After David and Naomi met, they spent a great deal of time together, sharing ideas and life stories. "Do you remember, David," said Naomi, "that restaurant where someone came over and asked if we were newlyweds? We couldn't stop talking to each other. This went on for hours and hours," she laughed. "It was crazy—we really couldn't stop. We finally reached a point where we could be quiet occasionally."

They became sexually involved after several weeks, both having been celibate for a long time. "His erections came slowly, but they worked," confided Naomi, "and, like the talking, we couldn't stop!"

According to Naomi, David was nervous about being sexually involved outside of marriage and was sure the neighbors saw and disapproved of his coming and going from her apartment. He decided they had to get married. Naomi had some doubts, particularly as to whether David's daughters would accept her, but she cared for David very much and was tired of living alone. So, married they were.

Because Jewish law decrees that marriage must wait a year following a spouse's death, they were first married by a judge in Naomi's apartment seven months after they met. Naomi recalled that it was Super Bowl Sunday, and the judge was late because he had been watching the game. The wedding guests didn't seem to mind tuning in before the ceremony. A more traditional Jewish wedding in the temple was held a few months later.

After they were married, David sold his house and moved into Naomi's apartment. He appears to have had no difficulty with this decision, as his big house was costly and difficult to maintain. After six years, they found a new home in a retirement community, where they have lived for eight years.

EDITH

 For any couple, finding and furnishing a new home together gives a deeply satisfying sense of belonging. It becomes their home instead of his or her home.

What Were Your Early Lives Like?

David

David was raised from infancy in an Orthodox Jewish orphanage after his parents were killed in an automobile accident. He had four siblings, from whom he was separated. Later in life he tried to locate them by every means possible, but with no success.

David left the orphanage at age 15 and joined the Civilian Conservation Corps, and later worked his way through college as a truck driver. He lived on his own until he married at 35.

Naomi

Naomi was four when her parents divorced. She and her older brother grew up in a Jewish neighborhood where divorce was unheard of. Thoroughly ashamed of her family's status, she lied and told her friends that her father was dead. Her mother worked in the garment industry and was very involved with the union. Explained Naomi, "My brother and I were an afterthought with her. She was there for us, but we weren't the big thing in her life. The big thing in her life was politics." Her mother wouldn't allow her father to visit when Naomi was a child, but as an adult she found him and stayed in touch until his death at age 99.

E D I T H

 Between her mother's political involvement and her father's absence, Naomi grew up very much on her own. I believe this has a good deal to do with her being the strong, independent woman she is today. I have worked with many women who appear to be tough on the outside but have a soft inner core that longs for the love and affection they lacked in childhood. I believe this is true of Naomi. David's orphaned childhood led to a deep, unmet need for a family. His insecurity grew out of the intensity of this need.

What Were Your Previous Relationships Like?

David

At the time of David's first marriage, he was working as a teacher in a yeshiva. His wife, Esther, had a 16-year-old daughter from a previous marriage, and they also had a daughter together. David noted, "Naomi takes care of me the way I took care of Esther. I did all the shopping and paid all the bills."

EDITH

 As a younger, healthier man, David had the caretaker role. Today, Naomi is very much in charge but finds the increased responsibility difficult at times. She knows David feels a loss of pride and control as he becomes more dependent on her. The gradual deterioration of health and memory will change the balance of power in a relationship and presents problems for both the caregiver and the care receiver.

David's wife was unwell for many years, and during the interview he became confused as to the cause of her illness and death. Naomi told me that Esther suffered from hepatitis that progressed to liver failure. Their sex life was infrequent because of Esther's poor health, yet David remained faithful to her throughout her life. It was an affectionate marriage, and he still misses her. There were tears in his eyes as he talked about her, although he does not, as a rule, share these feelings with Naomi. If Naomi speaks about her deceased husband, David gets angry and leaves the room.

EDITH

 David is jealous of Naomi's late husband. To feel some jealousy is normal, but to act on these feelings by walking out of the room closes the door literally and figuratively on Naomi and her willingness to share this part of her life with him. This limits the free exchange and closeness between them.

I, too, feel some jealousy when Jerry talks about his

late wife, but I know she was a part of his life for 45 years. It would be almost impossible for him to talk about his past without mentioning her, just as I cannot talk about my past without mentioning my husband of 35 years. Jerry also admits to some jealousy.

Although a certain amount of discomfort is to be expected, there cannot be genuine sharing if you must avoid discussing a huge chunk of your life. In fantasy, I would like to be the only person Jerry had ever loved, but it's just that—a fantasy. At one time or another, we all may have had similar fantasies but we must eventually accept the reality of past relationships. The past is part of each of us, and we need to bring our whole self into a new relationship.

Naomi

Naomi was wedded to her first husband for 26 years. They married when they were both 21 and had just graduated from college. His career as an architect was the reason they moved every few years. Although Naomi played the traditional role of homemaker while raising their two daughters, she loved to paint and had a studio in every house they lived in. She describes this marriage as "better than most." Her husband died suddenly of a heart attack, which made it particularly difficult for Naomi to accept the reality of his death. "I expected him home at any time," she reminisced.

EDITH

 This reaction is not at all unusual. Survivors frequently report sensing the presence of the deceased: A wife may turn around to "answer" a husband who is no

> longer there. For quite a few years after his death, I often found myself thinking thoughts in the very same words that my late husband used.
>
> When two people are close, they take on parts of each other. Now I sometimes hear Jerry's voice in my head, as gradually he becomes part of me.

Having gone directly from her mother's home into her long first marriage, Naomi found herself alone for the first time in her life after her husband's death. She "found being on my own to be one of the most exciting things that had ever happened to me." She managed an art gallery and dated frequently, but didn't want to make any personal commitments.

EDITH

 Working did a great deal for Naomi's self-esteem and helped her to cope with her grief. In the early stages of my own grieving process, therapy sessions with my clients were the only times I felt completely myself again. Working at a satisfying job is a good antidote to grief and a boost to self-esteem because pleasure, confidence, and pride come with accomplishment.

What Adjustments Have You Made in Your Relationship?

Naomi had been widowed and on her own for 18 years, while David had lived for 32 years with his first wife. To quote Naomi, "Living with another person, no matter whom, can be difficult, especially for someone like me who's been alone for so long. It took me ten years with David to say *we* instead of *me*."

Naomi had to adjust to David's feelings about other men. "He's jealous and insecure, but his behavior has gotten easier to live with." When we discussed this issue together, David said there were two men they saw at temple gatherings who paid a lot of attention to Naomi and whom he thought she liked in return. Naomi laughed and, with her New York accent, said, "Just one. There was another guy, but I dropped him. I don't even talk to him now when I see him—no big deal." She adjusted her behavior, which in turn gave David less cause for jealousy.

EDITH

 Naomi softens the dilemma of David's jealousy with humor. She protects David from the pain of his suspicions and herself from any possible accusations. To accept your partner's even casual friendship with someone of the opposite sex, you must be secure in your own self-worth. David's lonesome childhood did little to bolster his confidence. His declining health increased his neediness for Naomi, which most likely fed his fears of losing her, and, in turn, fueled his jealousy. With humor and a willingness to restrict her natural gregariousness, Naomi has decreased their conflicts around this issue.

David also made adjustments to please Naomi. He stopped his use of profanity and takes his hat off in the house. In view of David's upbringing, Naomi felt she had had to "civilize" him. In many ways, Naomi was in charge of this relationship.

What Do You Enjoy Doing Together?

For recreation and entertainment, the balance of power seems equal. David and Naomi make mutual decisions about recreation and social activities. They go to musical comedies together and enjoy big-band records and classical music. Naomi taught David to play Scrabble; he taught her card games. She plays table tennis with a group of women, and David plays pool with the husbands.

Until recently, David had been an enthusiastic golfer and fisherman. He has had to stop temporarily because of ill health. Naomi has a degree in fine art and has never stopped painting and taking art classes. She is quite talented and works in various media. At the end of my visit, I had the pleasure of seeing her studio and viewing her work. At present, she attends a weekly art group at the retirement community. This is one activity that Naomi feels is important enough to continue despite the increasing need to spend more time with David. David accepts this absence, which shows a flexibility in the relationship and a respect for their separate interests.

Moving Toward the Caretaker Role

David's over-all health and short-term memory have been steadily going downhill. Recent tests showed calcification in the brain. Sometimes David forgets what Naomi says five minutes after she says it. As I was leaving, David asked me to go out to dinner with them. I had to decline his kind offer since I had another appointment. He went on to ask me at least three more times as if he had never heard my answer. Naomi reminded David of my appointment and this seemed helpful to him. But when we discussed his forgetfulness, David was in denial.

EDITH

 It is frightening and disorienting to lose your memory, and David copes by pretending to himself that it isn't happening. Naomi is very aware of the problem and helps him when his short-term memory fails by filling in the gaps. By helping her husband in this way, she is gracefully adjusting to the caretaker role.

Seven years earlier, David had triple bypass surgery and a gallbladder operation. Shortly before my visit, he had had several incidents of fainting due to unknown causes, which kept him from driving, golfing, or fishing, for fear that he might pass out again. He had to stay home a great deal and wanted Naomi to stay with him. She told me frankly that she resented this, as it kept her from so much that she wanted to do.

EDITH

 Naomi's admission and acceptance of this resentment is healthy. Too many spouses secretly think this way, stay quiet, and feel guilty. But suppressed resentment often leaks out in the form of sarcasm or irritability.

To resent is not to stop loving or to stop doing what is necessary to care for your ailing mate. Although I believe I took good care of my first husband right up until the end, I had other feelings inside of me. In addition to experiencing the love and sadness, I was also an angry, resentful child who wanted to have fun and be cared for. But accepting this childlike part of myself made me more capable of functioning as a loving caretaker.

Despite her difficulty with the caretaker role, Naomi expressed her satisfaction with the marriage. "David's one of the sweetest guys you'll ever meet. Every day he tells me over and over 'I love you.' There's lots of physical affection, hugs and kisses, cuddling in bed. I think the average woman wants what I've got. I know he loves me. I've never doubted that for an instant."

Some Final Thoughts

At this point in their lives, Naomi and David are a good fit. Naomi is strong and takes care of David. Understandably, he somewhat resents her bossiness. But for the first time in his life, David is being nurtured and, in return, he gives Naomi the love and adoration she craves. This love and affection compensates Naomi for the many activities she has limited or given up so that she can care for David.

David and Naomi show us change is inevitable and that when one partner makes sacrifices to care for the other, feelings of resentment in the caretaker are *not* sinful. Love and affection *can* last.

CHAPTER 4

Committed True Love: Living Separately

Nancy and Pat

Nancy and Pat live in separate apartments in a retirement community. They have never considered marriage or living together. They have both closeness and some privacy, and this arrangement works well for them.

Late-Life Liberation

Both Nancy and Pat come from long, stable, conventional marriages, devoted to supporting and raising their families. Today, their separate living arrangements make for mutual joy when they reunite. As noted by Nancy, "Each time I see Pat after a few days of little or no contact, I experience the anticipation of going on a very special date."

With no children or jobs to tie them down, they add zest to their lives by traveling extensively. Now in their later years, they experience more freedom and adventure than ever before.

Introducing Nancy and Pat

Nancy is 75 years old and has been widowed for 16 years. Pat is nearly 77 and his wife passed away six years earlier. They are a very close, committed couple living in separate one-bedroom, one-bath apartments located about a mile apart. Both are Catholic and religion is very important to them, particularly for Nancy.

I first visited Nancy in her apartment where she had been living for only six weeks. It was as neat as a pin and pleasantly furnished with traditional pieces. Pictures of her children and grandchildren were proudly displayed, and on the refrigerator door were photos of Nancy and Pat together. I was particularly attracted by a snapshot taken on a hiking trail: Pat with a wooden staff in one hand and his other arm around Nancy. They looked happy.

Nancy is a tall, attractive woman with curly, graying hair. She greeted me warmly, and we sat at her dining room table to talk. Nancy has a delightful way of making fun of herself. She waves her hands and in a high-pitched voice laughingly talks about her children, who expect her to be "a good little mother and grandmother." I asked her if she meant that her role for years was as the "kind, sweet, all-giving Catholic mother" and that she is intimating, "I'm a different person now." Nancy agreed. Actually, Nancy is a practicing Catholic and a loving mother and grandmother, but her relationship with Pat has freed her to be, in many ways, a more liberated woman.

After conducting the interview with Nancy, I drove to Pat's apartment. The layout of the two apartments was identical, but they couldn't have looked more different. Pat's place was very cluttered, and the furniture was older and simpler. One entire wall was lined with books. In front of the couch was a large television set. Pat sat on the couch as we talked. He was casually dressed in shorts and a red T-shirt, with somewhat of a belly exposed beneath his shirt. He laughed frequently and heartily as we spoke.

How Did You Meet?

Nancy and Pat have known each other for 45 years. They both moved to the same suburban area as newlyweds. In the course of

Nancy's marriage, she had two children, while Pat and his wife had seven. They attended the same church, and gradually Nancy and Pat's wife Amanda became friends, carpooling their kids to the same parochial school. When her youngest child was in the third grade, Nancy obtained a position as a saleswoman for a local gift shop. Sometime later she found Amanda a job in the same store. In the 1950s, Nancy and Amanda formed an eight-woman support group that continued for more than a decade. When the group met at Amanda's home, Nancy would sometimes see Pat. She also saw him at church and at church functions, although the two couples did not socialize together. To Pat, Nancy was "just a pleasant lady I saw occasionally at my wife's support group."

How Did Your Relationship Develop?

Nancy retired from her job at the gift shop after 22 years. She wanted to write her family history and joined a memoir-writing class that Pat was already attending. By this time, Amanda was ill with breast cancer. Nancy promised Amanda she would drive Pat to their class and to his doctor appointments, as he was suffering from macular degeneration and cataracts and needed transportation.

After a two-year illness, Amanda passed away. Nancy became a hospice volunteer and, in that capacity, learned about the classic stages of grieving. A few months after Amanda's death, Pat asked her to go with him to see a movie. Nancy didn't know what to reply. She told a counselor at the hospice, "I just don't think he's grieving right." Her colleague replied, "Just be a friend." So she accepted Pat's invitation. From this time on, their relationship began to evolve into a genuine friendship.

Pat and Nancy continued with their writing class, had dinner out afterwards, and also went to the movies. Gradually they became physically affectionate—holding hands at the movies, exchanging a friendly hug, and kissing goodbye (a little longer if they'd been separated for a while). About six months after Amanda died, Pat and Nancy made love. To their surprise and delight, their sex life was more free and fulfilling than ever before. "I never in a thousand years believed I was capable of being so open and expressive sexually," Nancy exclaimed.

After they became sexually involved, Nancy and Pat remained in their respective homes but spent frequent nights together. This suited their different temperaments and living styles. As Pat said, "I never clutter up her house. She never complains about my mess, although she did make me clean up my bathroom." Pat once told Nancy, "If you want to get married, we'll get married." However, Nancy thought marriage would constrain her from leading her own life and spending her own money as she pleased. She and Pat have committed themselves to always being together and to taking care of each other if either becomes ill or disabled. This seems sufficient for them.

When the five-year project of her family memoirs was completed, Nancy felt a letdown. The winter rains came, and the house in which she had lived for 38 years felt too big. Pat also had a large house, which required extensive upkeep and had too many stairs. They agreed that a retirement community would better suit their needs.

Their homes sold quickly and netted them substantial financial gains. They were both recently established in their new homes at the time of my visit. The move into comparatively small apartments necessitated the disposal of much of their furniture. I asked Nancy if leaving her home of so many years, and letting go of so many possessions, was sorrowful for her. She said it wasn't. One factor that made the situation easier was that their children agreed to divide and share their parents' furniture. Thus, Pat and Nancy knew they would see their precious possessions again when they visited their families.

What Were Your Early Lives Like?

Nancy

Nancy grew up in a small community during the Depression. Her father was manager of a laundry. She had "a good, simple life." Her parents were affectionate, and she had two much-older aunts who lived nearby and were strict but loving toward her. Both of her parents are now dead, but she has one brother who has met Pat and gets along well with him.

EDITH

 Nancy's stable, happy childhood led to a sensible, secure adulthood. She was raised during the 1930s and '40s, when a woman's role was limited to being "a good little wife, mother, and grandmother." Today, Nancy *is* a "good" mother and grandmother, but she has the independence of mind to fashion a relationship with Pat that is very different from the conventional expectations of the era in which she was raised.

Pat

Pat was the eldest of three children. His father worked as a sales manager for a large manufacturing company after retiring from the military. In both capacities, he was forced to move his family frequently. Pat had difficulty making and keeping friends, and relied more on his own company and his love of books. He was close to and admired his father, but was distant from his mother, whom he described as "a chronic hypochondriac." As he says, "She always thought she was going to die of something." His mother came from a wealthy family, and the children were raised mostly by a housekeeper. Before the birth of his younger sister when he was ten years old, Pat was told that his mother was "going to be ill for a long time." Subsequently, he was left with his maternal grand-parents for a year. They paid little attention to him, and he took care of himself by reading from their extensive library.

As a young man, Pat had two years of college and then entered the army during World War II. When discharged, he traveled across the country, ending up on the West Coast. He held many different jobs, most of them in sales. His mother was disappointed that he did not finish his education and choose a "professional career."(Pat's brother had earned a Ph.D.) Both of his parents are now deceased, and his brother and sister are living in other states. Nancy has met them both, and she and Pat have traveled with his brother. Both of Pat's siblings have accepted his relation-ship with Nancy.

EDITH

 Pat's frequent moves as a child led to an early self–reliance. He became independent and adventurous, moved west, defied his family's expectations, and found work that suited him. He brings this sense of adven-ture into his relationship with Nancy. In her, he has found the loving, affectionate woman that his mother was not.

Their Long, Stable Marriages

Nancy

Nancy moved from her parents' home when she married at 23. Her husband was an accountant and made a good living. He was reliable, responsible, and took care of Nancy and their three chil-dren. She did not work outside the home until her youngest child was in the third grade. In fact, her husband offered her far more financial stability than Pat could have, so Pat might not have been right for her at this earlier stage of her life.

Nancy's husband was also more introverted and much less adventurous than Pat. Some of the challenging experiences Pat had with his young family would have been too frightening for her.

On the negative side, Nancy has mentioned that her husband was a worrier and "master of the put-down." True to her role as the uncomplaining wife, Nancy did not talk back, and the marriage was fairly conflict-free.

EDITH

 Resentment that is not expressed often leads to a lack of affection, spontaneity, and joy. When I look back on my first marriage, I realize that there were times when my irritated or sarcastic tone of voice had the same effect as a put-down. Although my husband said nothing, I believe now this resulted in less affection shown to me.

Nancy is careful not to make this mistake with Pat. Because of what she experienced in her marriage, she never puts Pat down for things like his messiness or disorganization. This frees them both to express more fully their affection and love.

Nancy's husband was ill for two years, and during his last six months they had the support of a hospice service. After his death, Nancy received additional comfort from her women's group. Just as important, she continued to work as a way of keeping her mind active and her body busy.

Pat

Pat met his future wife at a Catholic gathering for young people when he was 27 and she was 25. They married a few months later and eventually had seven children. He describes his marriage as a good one. Pat showed me a picture of himself and his wife from his memoirs. They were a handsome couple.

Pat's main conflict with his wife was over financial security. Working in sales sometimes meant weeks with no income. Pat told me, "During these periods, she thought we were going to die of starvation. I was completely confident we would be all right. Sometimes I'd go six weeks between jobs, and I'd have lots of fun doing all sorts of things, while she got madder and madder." They had arguments about what she thought were his "extravagances," such as the purchase of a rifle for a Mountain Man competition. She also worried a great deal about the children. Certainly seven children were a lot to worry about!

EDITH

 Pat was rebelling against some of the same negative traits he found in his mother, who, according to him, always thought her children "were about to die any minute." It is not uncommon to unconsciously choose a mate to repeat some of the patterns of childhood.

Pat and Nancy's comfortable financial circumstances make for more freedom from monetary concerns than during Pat's marriage. Nancy has her own income, and Pat is free to spend his retirement benefits as he pleases.

When Amanda died, it was "kind of a relief" to Pat after watching her suffer for two years. He went on a trip right after her death, admitting that "I didn't have much of a mourning period." He camped out and read *Huckleberry Finn*. He admits, "I wanted to do something different to occupy my mind. I really enjoyed myself."

EDITH

 It is not unusual for someone with a mate who has been ill for a long time to feel relief when death comes. A good deal of the mourning has been done during the illness. I am struck by Pat's ability to find pleasure in his own company, a skill he probably developed as a child in his grandparents' home. He found solace in reading then and again after his wife passed away.

What Problems Were Faced?
What Adjustments Were Made?

Nancy and Pat report very few problems, and it's possible that their separate living arrangement makes this possible. Certainly, living together would be difficult, with Nancy so neat and Pat so disorganized. When they visit each other, they are able to respect these differences: Pat doesn't clutter up Nancy's apartment and Nancy tolerates Pat's mess.

Their respect for each other's differences, and their ability to enjoy themselves with or without each other, makes for a smooth relationship. As Pat says, "I don't push her to do what she doesn't want to do, and she doesn't push me. If Nancy doesn't want to engage in an activity with me, I just do it alone, and she does the same."

But how can any couple avoid some degree of conflict? Perhaps the answer is that Nancy and Pat don't use the word "conflict." They say they have "heated discussions." An example is given in Chapter 18, *Personality Differences and Styles of Conflict*, page 193. See how their sense of humor and tolerance of each other's styles help to resolve this disagreement. Nancy knows that Pat is hot-tempered and this doesn't disturb her. Pat appreciates

Nancy's ability to calmly resolve the situation. Undoubtedly, they have had many other heated discussions that have been similarly resolved.

What Do You Value in Each Other?

Nancy describes Pat as easy going, affectionate, and kind. To her, "He is interesting—a historian, always ready for a new adventure. And he is a wonderful lover!"

Pat likes Nancy's good nature. He finds her pleasant, never moody or sharp. "How could you not like Nancy?" he asked. Pat showed me his finished memoirs. On the first page of the book, he has a dedication: "To Nancy, dear critic and editor." Pat continued, "I enjoy being with Nancy no matter what we're doing, even in a house fire." They both laughed, and Nancy added, "He'd save me."

What Are Your Daily and Weekly Routines?

Both Pat and Nancy prefer to live separately and continue the same routines they had in their previous homes. Each values their independent time apart and spends Monday through Wednesday evenings on their own. Pat likes to watch a movie every night. Nancy washes her hair, writes letters, pays bills, and phones friends. When Thursday arrives, they are excited and happy to see each other.

They alternate staying at each other's apartment. In the evening, they enjoy a glass of wine together (they both like Gewürztraminer), watch the news, and eat dinner on trays in front of the television. At Nancy's house, she cooks dinner, washes the dishes, and makes breakfast the next morning. Pat takes over these jobs at his house. The one who is visiting gets the first section of the newspaper at breakfast.

Their routine includes the chore of paying bills. Although they each have their own expenses, Nancy handles Pat's bills in addition to her own as he tends to fall behind with his payments. He appreciates her help. Nancy also helps Pat keep track of his appointments, as he has begun to have some difficulty with his memory.

EDITH

 Memory problems are very common as we grow older. I struggle with memory myself. The name of a person, a book, or a place just vanishes from my mind when I need it, but will return later if I relax and don't strain to search for it.

What Are Your Interests and Activities?

At home together, they enjoy television, although their tastes differ. Nancy prefers dramas, especially British productions, while Pat likes Westerns. They compromise and take turns watching both kinds of programs. They also have different tastes in movies. Nancy often goes without Pat to films that only she would enjoy.

EDITH

 This ability to respect and consider each other's preferences contributes another important factor to the success of this relationship.

Pat has a multitude of hobbies. He grew up with guns and competed as a sharpshooter for many years. This coincided with his love of American history, as evidenced by a bookcase filled with history books, chronologically arranged from the American Revolution to the present. In addition to his memoirs, Pat has written an unpublished novel set during the Civil War. He enjoys carpentry and, along with one of his sons, made the attractive redwood-stump table in his living room. When he becomes more established in the retirement community, he plans to join the camera club, the writing club, the hiking club, and to use the woodworking shop.

Every year Nancy and Pat take two or three trips with their tent trailer. They've been to Hawaii, Alaska, and last year they crossed the country, traveling 7,500 miles. They went to Europe on the anniversary of the Battle of the Bulge during W.W. II, as Pat had been a paratrooper with the 101ST Airborne. When I interviewed them, they were planning a two-month visit to Italy. Nancy really appreciates traveling with Pat. Her husband was prone to lose his temper when things went wrong. In contrast, Pat doesn't get upset; when the wheel came off of their camper, he merely fixed it. Pat says of traveling with Nancy, "We have fun. She's the person with whom I can do everything I want to do."

Some Final Thoughts

Nancy and Pat are a shining example of late-life liberation. Nancy had been a conventional wife and mother, but today has the flexibility to maintain a different lifestyle and enjoys a romantic and sexual relationship with a man to whom she is not married. Pat is able to more freely express his adventurous nature now that he has reached the stage of life when he no longer needs to raise and financially support seven children. They have chosen to live separately and, for Nancy and Pat, this gives them the freedom they desire after their long, responsibility–filled marriages. Their lifestyles might not be for everyone, but for Nancy and Pat it makes for a happy and deeply committed partnership.

CHAPTER 5

With a 26-Year Age Difference, Can There Be a Successful Union?

Donna and Stuart

"He was 78 years old, and I thought I didn't want to get involved with an older man. I wanted someone closer to my age. But no one else was around."

"After 56 years with my first wife, I have learned how to handle a woman; how to keep her loving me. Not a day goes by now that I don't put my arms around Donna a dozen times and tell her how much I love her."

The Balance of Power in a Very Traditional Marriage

Both Donna and Stuart come from conservative Christian backgrounds. In this loving relationship, their religion defines their roles; the man is the head of the household and the woman follows his lead. Earlier in their marriage, the 26-year age difference reinforced these roles. Today, Stuart needs Donna's help and, as Donna grows more and more self-confident, the balance of power is gradually shifting to a more equal union.

Introducing Donna and Stuart

Donna is 64 years of age and Stuart is 90. They have been married for 12 years. We sat talking around their dining room table. Donna is a sweet, friendly woman with short, gray hair, dressed neatly in pants and a colorful blouse. Stuart is heavy-set with a powerful chest and a strong, steady gaze. As we talked, they laughed and touched each other.

They live in a house Donna owns on five acres of land in a rural development. It is nestled among tall oak trees with a rolling lawn leading down to a picturesque abandoned barn. The porch is full of flower pots and bird feeders. Near the barn is a deer feeding station filled with corn. At night, with the help of a bright porch light, Stuart and Donna can see as many as ten deer feeding. They both love animals, but the feeder keeps the deer away from the house where they would eat the roses. Donna told me that once a bear came to the front of the house at 3:00 in the afternoon but went to the deer feeder and spent nearly an hour eating. The two of them enjoyed watching from behind the safety of their living room window.

Their home contains many pieces of fine, antique furniture that Stuart brought from his house to supplement Donna's furnishings. The rooms are crowded with numerous knick-knacks and the walls are lined with religiously themed plaques.

How Did You Meet?

Donna had been a part-time volunteer at the local history center for some years. She particularly enjoyed taking elementary school students through the attractive exhibits and dramatically telling stories about people and events during the early years of the area. Ordinarily somewhat shy and reserved, Donna felt free to fully express herself with children. On display was a small working model that showed how gold was extracted and refined from ore in the region. Being quite old, it often malfunctioned. After a serious breakdown, Donna wanted to find someone who would volunteer to overhaul the machinery.

After asking a friend, she heard about Stuart, who lived in a nearby small community and had the skills and tools to do the job. She contacted him. Yes, he would look at the equipment, but he needed to have the model taken to his house because he was caring for his terminally ill wife. This was done and, after a time, Stuart got the machine operating properly. The exhibit was reinstalled at the history center and worked satisfactorily for a while, but one of the parts broke down again. With Stuart's directions, Donna removed the part and took it back to his house for repair.

Then one day, Stuart phoned Donna to tell her that his wife had passed away. Donna expressed her sympathy and they talked for a long time. Thereafter, whenever Stuart was feeling lonely, he called Donna and they talked.

How Were You Attracted to Each Other?

Donna saw Stuart as a good Christian, and a unique man. He did not use bad language, nor did he smoke or drink. His extensive traveling for his profession made him fascinating to be with.

Stuart liked Donna's enthusiasm about the history center and, whenever he visited, he observed her dramatic performances with the students. "She can be so outgoing and lively, but also so soft and gentle." Stuart also appreciated her physical attractiveness, her sensitivity, and her high sense of values.

How Did Your Relationship Develop?

After Stuart had phoned her a few times, Donna remembered that she had seen an extensive collection of books on California history in his house. Feeling lonely herself, she started visiting with him frequently and together they discussed history while looking through his books. Both of them enjoyed this togetherness, and little by little their relationship grew. As Donna said,

"From his conversation, I could tell where it was going. He was getting serious."

During one visit, Stuart showed Donna a full-length mink cape that had been his wife's. She put it on, admiring it in a mirror, saying, "I feel elegant." Stuart replied, "You look elegant. If we were of the same religious persuasion, I would ask you to be my wife." Coming just two months after his wife's death, this seemed too soon for Donna. They continued seeing each other, visiting each other's homes, having dinners together, and going to services at each other's churches. Then one evening at Stuart's house, Donna remarked, "It's so nice to have someone to come home to." Stuart then came over to her and gave her a hug and their first kiss. From then on, they dated more often and Stuart talked again about marriage. They each strongly believed that there should be no sexual activity between them until marriage.

As their relationship developed, Donna had some mixed thoughts. "I wanted to marry him, yet because of our age difference (she was 52 and he was 78), I didn't want to get involved with an older man again. There had been an age difference of 34 years between me and my first husband. I wanted someone closer to my own age, but there was no such man around. I didn't want a divorced man or one who had never been married because I didn't want all that baggage, nor did I want a man so set in his ways and habits that he might be unwilling to change."

Another important issue for Donna was the fact that she had recently been laid off from her part-time secretarial position, and with no income, her savings were almost gone. In addition to their romantic feelings for each other, there was also the practical reality of the expense of two households. So they decided to be married and live in Donna's house. Some friends thought this was too fast, since the wedding would take place only ten months after Stuart's wife had passed away, following her seven years of illness.

EDITH

 Many people do not understand that years of caring for an ill spouse are years when the need for love and companionship are not being fulfilled. Also, during a long illness there is ample time for preliminary grieving and preparing for the loss, so that there need not be a period of time set by convention for a new relationship to start.

The wedding ceremony took place in a private chapel in Las Vegas and then Donna and Stuart honeymooned in Hawaii. Donna, who has a delightful sense of humor, told me the following story about their wedding. She had prepared their vows and a tape recording of a friend playing the organ and singing *"Where Thou Goest I Will Go."* A young couple with a nine-month-old baby, who had just been married in the chapel, were witnesses to their wedding. The ceremony was interrupted periodically by the baby's cries, which together with the playing of Donna's recording, resulted in a longer period than was standard for a Las Vegas wedding. During this time, the chapel photographer kept popping in and out, looking at his watch. But the vows and the music went as planned and, despite the interruptions, Donna and Stuart had a lovely wedding.

What Were Your Early Lives Like?

Donna

Donna is from a family originally consisting of three sons and one daughter. One brother died in infancy and, with Donna being much younger than her two surviving brothers, her parents were very protective of her. She had a lonely childhood, with not much affection being shown to her by her parents or brothers. In high school, she studied clerical skills and held secretarial positions during much of her adult working years. Her upbringing was strict, and she received much verbal abuse, mainly from her mother. As a result, Donna describes herself as having low self-esteem, poor confidence, and a tendency to downgrade herself.

Since she had few opportunities to socialize with men, when a friend of the family did show an interest in her, she quickly married him as a way to leave home. She was 34 years younger than her husband and her mother strongly objected to the marriage. When Donna's father and mother died, her two brothers managed to acquire most of the family's assets, leaving little for Donna. In recent years, she has had contact with her brothers. They like Stuart and have given her some of her mother's jewelry and household items.

EDITH

 Donna was so confined and controlled as a young woman that the only man she could meet was a family friend who visited the home. Being married to a much older man reinforced the childlike role she assumed in her family of origin. In this role it was difficult for her to fight her more powerful older brothers for her rightful inheritance. Also, her low self-esteem made Donna somewhat submissive during the early part of her marriage to Stuart. But over the years, she has gradually learned to express her needs and desires.

Stuart

Stuart was one of eight children in a close-knit family. He had a wonderful childhood with many interesting activities. An adventurous lad, Stuart left home at age 18, joined the merchant marine, and traveled around the world. After he returned home he went to college and earned a degree as a chemical engineer.

Stuart was employed for many years by a petroleum company, often traveling to the company's overseas facilities. At age 60, he retired from full-time work but continued consulting in foreign countries until age 65.

What Were Your Previous Relationships Like?

Donna

When Donna met her first husband, she was 26 and he was 60. He was a calm, quiet, easy-going man, and they had a good relationship. After 25 years of marriage, he died from pneumonia. They had no children, although Donna had always wanted to be a mother. A medical misdiagnosis had resulted in a hysterectomy that prevented pregnancy.

Stuart

Stuart married at age 21, and this marriage lasted for 56 years. He had one daughter and two sons. His marriage was also a good one. His wife was ill with cancer for seven years and died shortly before his relationship with Donna began.

What Adjustments Have You Made?

It is interesting to follow the fluctuations in the balance of power in this relationship. As with most traditional marriages of older folks, Donna and Stuart's marriage is, for the most part, male controlled. Not only custom and religious convictions have supported Stuart's dominance in the relationship, but because he holds the purse strings, he has the final veto over major financial decisions. For example, Donna would like to sell Stuart's house and put the proceeds toward a larger home. This would allow her to have more space for their things, including a separate office area for herself. She believes, as she said, "It would be easier to take care of a larger home." When I asked Stuart about this idea, he replied that Donna would not be able to care for a larger home as she got older. That seemed to settle the matter.

Donna receives Social Security benefits and earns some money by freelancing secretarial services. As she puts it, "I can use this money for things I want that Stuart doesn't think I need."

EDITH

 It is good that Donna has a small income of her own. It gives her at least some independence. Money is an important determinant of power in any relationship.

One thing that required special attention was the maintenance of an acceptable temperature in their house. Stuart never seemed to feel either hot or cold. It took some time for Donna to make him aware that she felt cold most of the time, and that a suitable fire should be maintained in the living room fireplace. It took sometime and repeated complaints from her, but he finally learned to accommodate her need for warmth.

Another major conflict in the beginning was that Stuart never seemed to get hungry, getting by on one or, at the most, two meals a day. On the other hand, Donna frequently felt hungry or even "starved," as Stuart did not suggest that it was time to eat. Gradually as Donna learned to make her needs known, Stuart listened, and they now have meals at regular times.

Before their marriage Donna had a number of dogs and cats in the house and on the grounds. At one time she considered her three cats as her "babies." Stuart was both allergic to the cats and uncomfortable with them. Despite this Donna told him, "I've had them longer than I've had you!" Now Donna has only one cat, who is still her "baby" and very important to her. Stuart has managed to overcome his allergy and he even likes this cat and takes care of it when Donna is away from home.

Donna and Stuart have compromised equally in many areas. At the very beginning of their marriage, Stuart made the first major concession by giving up his home for Donna's. They each had a complete household's worth of furnishings, and it was very difficult for them to part with many objects that would not fit into one house. Thus, they each gave up some much-loved possessions. Even now, their house feels cluttered because each of them kept certain items with which they could not part, as is often the case with many older couples.

And of course, there are all the habits of a lifetime that people have to learn about each other. Donna is disturbed when Stuart leaves the kitchen light on, does not close the toilet seat cover, or doesn't wash dishes to her satisfaction. He has gradually learned to turn off the lights and close the toilet cover, but Donna does the dishes more often!

EDITH

 If something is particularly important to you, as clean dishes are to Donna, it is often best to take care of it yourself.

Sometimes Stuart thinks that Donna spends too much money on unnecessary items. She likes to stock up on household supplies because the local stores are a good distance from their house and buying extras gives her a secure feeling. They argue about this, and Donna says she never wins.

EDITH

 In actuality, she does win but doesn't realize it. Stuart doesn't agree with her, but he doesn't actually stop her from shopping. Like Donna, women throughout history have gained their power in subtle ways, often without acknowledging it even to themselves.

As Stuart slows down with age, Donna supports him in many more ways than she would like him to know. This is beginning to change the balance of power in this marriage. For example, she has done all the driving for the past three years, as Stuart is now unable to drive as a result of his general weakness. He finds it hard to accept that his physical strength is waning, and although Donna helps him with such chores as bringing in the wood and clearing the yard, she doesn't make a point of it. This protects his pride as he grows more dependent upon her.

What Are Your On-going Activities?

This couple enjoys many activities, sharing responsibilities and pleasures on a fairly equal basis. In the past, because of Stuart's extensive experiences overseas, they took tours to European and South American countries. But now with Stuart having difficulty walking, such trips are over. Donna helps their church with secretarial services and Sunday School teaching. Stuart continues to be proud of her abilities. He assists at the church's second-hand store.

At home, they read the Bible and other sacred publications, watch conservative television programs together, and enjoy playing dominos. They joke together with few inhibitions.

They have many friends from their church with whom they have weekly potluck lunches. Also, they still have a few remaining friends from each one's previous marriage. Donna likes to show pictures of her early family and her first husband. Stuart has no problem with this.

Donna appreciates Stuart's warmly expressed affection. He reminisces, "After 56 years with my first wife, I have learned how to handle a woman to keep her loving me. Not a day goes by now that I don't put my arms around Donna a dozen times and tell her how much I love her. I never go to bed without kissing her and wishing her a good sleep."

Some Final Thoughts

This marriage is what I would term complementary, because Stuart's and Donna's personalities seem to complement each other. Stuart is a very strong, assertive man and, despite his advanced age, is very much in charge of the household. This, and his frequently expressed affection, fulfills Donna's needs to be loved and cared for. Their strong conservative religious beliefs, and both their upbringings, support the male-dominated balance of this marriage.

With Donna's very sheltered childhood, she is able to accept the more submissive role, though not without some discomfort and some assertion of her own needs, such as keeping her cat and stocking up on food. Because she is so much younger than Stuart, whose strength is beginning to fail, she is able to care for him in physical ways, such as driving the car and bringing in wood for the fireplace. Thus, the balance of power is changing somewhat as Stuart ages and he becomes more dependent on Donna. With their loving respect for and consideration of each other, this marriage continues to be a satisfactory one for them both.

CHAPTER 6

It's Not All Peaches and Cream, but They're Doing Better!

Ellen and Ralph

They met through a personal ad. After ten months, they married and moved into his home. Two-and-a-half months after their wedding, they recognize the need to make adjustments. What are the problems they face? How are they attempting to overcome them? Let's look at their ongoing efforts for success.

The Importance of Constructive Problem-Solving

All couples have some degree of conflict between them. Ellen and Ralph have been able to look at the ways their conflicts develop, show understanding for each other's situations and feelings, and take responsibility for their own behavior. This constructive problem-solving needs to be a continuing process in all successful relationships, older-couple or otherwise.

Introducing Ellen and Ralph

From the outside it looked like a large hotel set in an exclusive suburb. Upon entering its elegantly furnished foyer, I was greeted by the doorman. He phoned Ellen, who a few minutes later, ushered me into a spacious apartment where, over morning tea, our interview commenced.

I didn't meet Ralph until later that afternoon, when Ellen introduced me to him, prior to my interviewing him alone. Seeing them together, I was struck by what an attractive pair they were. They looked as if they had just walked off a movie set, playing a typical older American couple. Both Ellen and Ralph are tall and slim, with full heads of white hair, Ellen's elegantly coifed. She wore a stylish, full-length yellow dress, and Ralph looked most handsome in well-tailored slacks and a short-sleeved summer shirt.

Ellen is 62 years old; Ralph is 69. Both are employed full time, Ellen as a real estate agent and Ralph as an insurance adjuster, though he was between jobs when we met. They are an example of a couple who, having been together just a little more than a year, are still in the working-out phase of their relationship. They have learned from past mistakes and have the intelligence and knowledge to look objectively at the difficulties in their relationship and to take steps to improve it.

How Did You Meet?

Both Ellen and Ralph had previous marriages. They were now at a time in their lives when each was motivated to find a new partner with whom to spend their remaining years. Ellen had placed a notice in the personal column of her local newspaper, stating that she was "a 61-year-old female, with a good sense of humor, interested in meeting a gentleman in his sixties who desires living in a recreational vehicle and traveling with his partner."

During an airplane flight, Ralph talked with a psychologist sitting next to him about his interest in meeting a woman. The psychologist suggested that he look through the personal ads in the newspaper. The phone call from Ralph was one of three that Ellen received in her phone mailbox.

After a follow-up phone conversation, Ellen agreed to meet with Ralph for the standard cup of coffee. She felt that such a meeting would be safe and, if necessary, brief. However, it wasn't brief for Ellen and Ralph.

A few days later they went to a movie together. It was so bad they walked out and went to dinner. Things seemed to be going right between them, as they talked for *four hours* over their food! A few days later Ellen asked Ralph to drive with her to visit a friend in a nearby city. He felt it was a real compliment to be asked to meet a friend so soon and happily agreed to go.

How Were You Attracted to Each Other?

Ellen saw Ralph as a handsome man who was easy to talk to, with a calm manner and a sense of humor. Ralph was attracted to Ellen by her good looks and a manner that demonstrated intelligence, sensitivity, competence, and a caring attitude. Ellen pointed out that in many ways, she and Ralph, in both looks and interests, "are reflections of ourselves."

Beyond these physical and intellectual characteristics, they discovered similarities in their backgrounds and interests. They were both brought up on Midwestern farms and have similar ethical standards. Ellen has three children and Ralph has four. Equally important was their mutual desire to travel, and eventually live in a large RV. In fact, this was probably the "clincher" for them.

How Did Your Relationship Develop?

Ellen and Ralph, who were both working full time when they met, depended on the telephone in order to stay in contact during the week. Sometimes their conversations lasted as long as three hours. They saw each other on weekends, engaging in many different activities together, and visiting each other's homes.

Two months after meeting, they became sexually involved, and four months later they agreed to live together in Ralph's larger apartment condominium, this despite the fact that Ellen had to commute 45 minutes to work each day. A striking example of their compatibility was that Ellen thought she could have chosen most of Ralph's furnishings herself. She simply added some of her own furniture, and she was ready to move in. Ralph allowed her to do whatever she wished in the apartment to help her feel at home.

Each of them understood that, considering their ages, and the fact that they "had been around the block a few times," they both knew they were starting on a serious, long-term relationship that included marriage. In Ralph's words, "We didn't want to wait!"

During our discussion, I asked this question: "What were your reasons for getting married, rather than just continuing to live together." These were their answers:

Ralph: "This is a long-term commitment for both of us, rather than just a relationship of convenience. In marriage we are more committed to resolve differences so that our union lasts."

Ellen: "He fills a spot for me that has been empty for many years. I feel that life becomes much more meaningful with marriage, and there is a purpose now beyond just existence."

Four months after starting to live together, Ellen and Ralph were married in Hawaii.

What Were Your Previous Relationships Like?

Ellen

Ellen had three previous marriages. She was first married at age 20. This lasted for 11 years and they had three children. Eventually her husband became an alcoholic and physically abusive. After ten years, Ellen remarried. This union lasted for two-and-a-half years, ending when her husband died from a sudden heart attack. While not an ideal husband, he was good with her children. His unexpected death was difficult for her.

Following this marriage, Ellen developed a relationship with a friend of her second husband, and they married after a year. Their marriage was more of a good friendship than a love match. It lasted for six months, and as Ellen said, "Without love, no matter how hard we tried, our marriage had no fulfilling aspects." It ended with a mutual divorce.

For the next 16 years, Ellen lived alone, although she had some passing relationships. It was during this period that she became financially self-supporting in various occupations, including property management, marketing, and real estate.

Ralph

Ralph also had three previous marriages. The first one, at age 26, was to a woman who later developed breast cancer that remained untreated until Ralph insisted that she see a doctor. The irony was that she was a registered nurse. After six years of what was proving to be a good marriage, with four children, Ralph's first wife passed away. Six months after his wife's death, he married a much younger woman. A widower with four children, Ralph now admits that he entered this marriage out of desperation. His new wife was far too young and inexperienced to be a stepmother to his children. After four difficult months, they divorced.

Ralph married for the third time five years later. During this period, he was a bus driver and was required to be away from home much of the time. This absence affected the marriage, which ended after four years.

What Problems Were Faced and What Adjustments Were Made?

When Ellen and Ralph first met, they just "clicked" with each other. Many things seemed to match between them, providing a good start for their relationship. Their positive attitude continued as they lived together and then married. Now, within the last six months, some problems have arisen.

Ellen, in addition to her 45-minute commute to work each way, puts in many hours of work selling real estate, including evenings and weekends. She often comes home quite exhausted and, understandably, she wants more help from Ralph.

In recent months, Ralph had changed jobs, and at the time of our interview, was in the middle of a three-week period between positions. Job security formed an essential part of Ralph's self-esteem. Even with a new position in sight, the lay-off period was negatively affecting him. In addition, he had gone through a traumatic operation for cancer, which left him stressed and with some degree of depression. The depression affected his ability to be as fully active and involved as Ellen would have liked.

Ellen's Perspective

Ellen: "Over the past six months, I've become more responsible for housekeeping, chores, making purchases, cooking dinners, social activities. This was not true when we first started dating and then began living together. But lately I resent having to handle all these responsibilities alone."

EDITH

 It is good that Ellen is aware of her resentment so she can express it directly to Ralph rather than indirectly or in hurtful ways such as withdrawal or sarcasm.

Ellen: "Ralph is between jobs. He may be depressed and insecure as to where he is going. I am cast in the leadership role because I'm so competent, but my husband is extremely competent himself. He's capable of doing as much as I can. I would like him to take more responsibility on his part and also initiate activities together with me."

EDITH

 Here Ellen shows understanding of Ralph's probable depression. The ability to sense and appreciate your spouse's underlying emotions is extremely important. Instead of putting down Ralph, she gives him credit for being competent. She's clear about what she wants.

Ralph's Perspective

Ralph: "She has very definite feelings about how she wants to be treated."

EDITH

 Ellen is clear about what she wants, and he hears her—a good sign.

Ralph: "I attribute ulterior motives to what she says."

EDITH

 He is aware that he is attributing. In other words, he knows that Ellen may or may not have "ulterior motives."

Ralph: "Maybe we should have waited longer to be married to better understand each other."

EDITH

 They could have had a longer period of living together to work out problems before marriage.

> Whether living together or married, couples usually need some time to make the initial adjustments, and Ellen and Ralph strongly wanted the commitment of marriage.

Working Things Out

I first interviewed Ellen and Ralph separately. The next morning, I met with them together. During the previous evening, they had obviously begun to work on their problems. Each one made a number of frank and sincere statements that included the following:

Ellen: "When we get into an argument, we must decide how we're going to work things out. Part of solving an argument is to bond and create an intimacy together. Both of us understand that because we are such independent personalities, we can become brutal verbally, which could destroy our marriage. Therefore, we have to find a way to change. One way is through some type of signal to indicate that a dangerous blowup is coming, then separating until we calm down.

We certainly have similar goals, and one thing I've noticed about Ralph is that when he knows how I feel about something, he will do anything to make things better between us. It's hard for him to read my mind when all he sees or hears is an emotional reaction from me. I must consciously overcome that behavior."

EDITH

> Ellen gives Ralph credit for wanting to please her, and she also takes responsibility for her own actions. She knows she must control her emotions. Ellen needs to state her point clearly when she is calmer. And she's right—no one can read minds.

Ellen: "I love him very much, and I am very committed to do

anything I can to make this a successful marriage, but I can't do it by myself. I know he's also very committed to our relationship but I need him to reassure me of that."

EDITH

 We all need reassurance that we are loved and that the relationship is of prime importance. Ellen is openly asking for reassurance and giving Ralph credit for his commitment to her.

Ralph: "I've had bad situations before and don't want them to happen again. Sometimes my baggage from previous relationships makes me suspicious. I must learn not to let previous relationships and baggage from the past affect this relationship."

EDITH

 In wishing to be less hurt when Ellen explodes, Ralph takes responsibility for his reaction and acknowledges that he needs to take more control over his emotions. It is more constructive to understand and change your own responses than to try to change your partner's behavior.

Ralph: "We say things in anger to each other that can be hurtful. She internalizes things that come bubbling out later. They often have no importance or real meaning and I must learn not to take them so seriously. Ellen is absolutely right. We must stop such brutal arguments, because at some point, they could tip us over the edge, and neither of us wants that."

EDITH

 In my work with couples, I give rules for arguing. They need to learn *not* to threaten to leave and *not* to call

each other unkind names. Ellen and Ralph are learning such rules and are starting to take a "time out" if
they think they are losing control. Without such rules,
hurt and bitterness can build up and threaten a marriage. Ralph's statement shows an understanding of
this danger.

Ralph: "I am really convinced Ellen internalizes things until
they get to the point at which they explode. If she could tell me
at the time when I am insulting, demeaning, irritating, or disre-
spectful of her, that would be a big help. I would then be able to
cope with it right then."

EDITH

 Ralph is also willing to admit that he can be insulting
and he hits on another key point: Rather than let hurt
and anger build up slowly, it is important to express
what disturbs you as soon as possible in a non-blaming way. Ellen could say to Ralph, using an "I" statement, "I feel hurt by your tone of voice. Could you say
that to me in a different way?"

Ralph: "Both of us love each other enough to do what's necessary to get past some of these blocks and make this relationship
work."

EDITH

 This mirrors Ellen's last statement about commitment.
Both of them want to make the marriage work and to
have a good understanding of the problems in their
interactions.

Some Final Thoughts

Ellen and Ralph are an excellent example of the early adjustment stage, common in most new relationships. When interviewed, they had not known each other for as long a time as had many of the other couples described in this book. They still needed time to understand and accommodate to each other's needs and personalities. Of course, it is a bit arbitrary to ascribe the working out of problems to an early adjustment stage only. Life is continually changing, especially as we age. (**Naomi** and **David's** situation is a good example of this.)

I contacted Ellen and Ralph sometime after our interview and learned that they were still actively involved in constructive problem-solving. And very recently, a postcard from them, while traveling and permanently living in their motor home, reads, "We're enjoying our retirement and continuing to make adjustments."

The process of constructive problem-solving never stops. It includes clear communication, careful listening to your partner, and striving to understand his or her point of view. Also important are stating your own desires in a clear, non-blaming way, and taking responsibility for your own motivations, feelings, and behaviors. All of this, Ellen and Ralph continue to do. With their love for each other and their determination to make their marriage work, they are well on their way to a good life together.

CHAPTER 7

She's Ten Years Older, and It's Working Fine

Gayle and Jim

Can age make a difference? Gayle and Jim say it affects the people around them more than it affects them. A friend of Jim's once asked, "She's a lot older than you, isn't she?" Jim replied, "If *I* were older than *she*, you'd never ask that question."

Thank the Goddess, They Found Each Other

Both Gayle and Jim, who are spiritual in an unconventional sense, appealed to their guiding spirits for a mate and received what they asked for. Gayle told her Goddess specifically what she wanted in a man, and so was able to recognize Jim when he walked in the door.

Knowing what you really want in a partner, and not being willing to settle for less, can sometimes, in a magical way, bring you what you desire.

Gayle and Jim met me on a country road to guide me to their house five miles away. It was a winding, hilly, bumpy drive over dirt roads through rocky California foothills that were just beginning to turn green from the winter rains. About the time I began wondering, "How far must it be?" there appeared a large, gracious redwood house, surrounded by trees, beside a creek, and with smoke curling up from the chimney.

The house is open and spacious, with high ceilings, hardwood floors, and a large rock-faced fireplace. A broad deck overlooks the creek and rocky, oak-covered hills. A few of Gayle's metal sculptures are displayed inside and outside the house.

Introducing Gayle and Jim

Gayle, a 59-year-old widow, is a sculptor and the owner of a small art gallery. She is of medium height, with silver hair and an open, friendly, talkative manner. She was dressed in jeans and a colorful shirt over which she wore an attractive beaded necklace.

Jim, ten years younger and divorced, is a writer, freelance editor, and skilled in computers. He also is of medium height, with brown hair and eyes and a ruddy, smiling face. He was dressed casually in colorful pants and a T-shirt.

Lively and affectionate, Gayle frequently touched Jim's arm or leg and kissed him on the cheek and Jim smiled at her lovingly.

The acreage on which the house sits is owned by Gayle. In addition to the house, Gayle has a studio in which she creates metal and stone sculptures. Gayle and Jim live there together and are planning to get married in six months. As our conversation started, I could hear soft, classical music coming from speakers mounted high on the walls.

How Did You Meet?

One morning, five years ago, Gayle was in her art gallery and Jim came in. She spent about two hours telling him about the displays and the gallery operation. When lunchtime came, he agreed to pick up lunch for them, and they continued talking. Finally he purchased some art as gifts and made a phone call to some friends in the community whom Gayle also knew. Gayle thought, "I think this guy is flirting with me. He looks very, very cute and certainly is younger than me."

The friends he called came to the gallery and, much to Gayle's surprise, Jim warmly hugged the lady. According to Gayle, "He did it very nicely. I'd better not let him out of my sight!"

At the same time, Jim thought to himself, "I want to know her better than just as a proprietor of a gallery."

Gayle invited their mutual friends to dinner a month later and also asked Jim to come. She prepared a sumptuous dinner. Jim brought wine, and Gayle observed how well he interacted with everyone. As Gayle knew that Jim was skilled with computers, she asked him for help with one she had recently acquired. He happily agreed to help her.

What Attracted You to Each Other?

Gayle had lived alone since her husband's death, and she became lonely, wanting to share her life with someone. Being a devotee of the ancient Greek Goddess Minerva, at two o'clock one morning, with a full moon in sight, Gayle climbed a special hill near her house to ask her Goddess for help.

She asked for someone to love, someone who would love her, but just not anyone. Her Goddess then asked what she was looking for and Gayle replied, "A man who is not a drinker or smoker, intelligent, educated, open-minded. Since I've accomplished a lot in my life, I don't want someone threatened by my successes, but who will be delighted with what I've accomplished. He should like animals and be kind to dogs and cats. He should be self-sufficient and not want me to care for him at this stage of life. While comfortable with me, he should have his own interests in life, be nurturing, compassionate, and with no hang-ups about sex. Finally, he should be concerned about the community in which we live."

Gayle found the following qualities in Jim: "He has a wonderful, open, smiling face with lively eyes. He's a warm person. He doesn't seem to be a 'game player.' He doesn't try to impress me with his work or his previous relationships with women. He seems self-sufficient and has his own interests in life. He is a compassionate person, very trusting, open, and honest."

Jim described what he found so attractive in Gayle: "Her liveliness and enthusiasm. The way she approaches life. She's very positive. I feel no age difference in her presence."

EDITH

 You might want to write down the traits that are important to you, as suggested in Chapter 25, *Examining What You Want in a Partner*. To protect yourself from becoming involved with the wrong person, it is just as important to recognize such traits and behaviors that are opposite of those that Gayle observed in Jim, such as "game playing," boasting, and being overly dependent on others.

How Did Your Relationship Develop?

After the first dinner party, Jim came from the city to Gayle's house to give her some help with her computer. As Gayle recounted, "When Jim entered my house, my dog, who never shows an interest in any man, went right over to him. When he kneeled down to pet her, she actually licked his face. I've never seen that before! Then, to top it off, my cat, who is also very independent, went to his chair, allowing him to pick her up. I thought that this fellow really had something special!"

"We had a five-hour visit that evening," Gayle continued. "When he left, he gave me a hug. It felt very good."

Gayle didn't hear from Jim for a month. Then she received an attractive hand-designed thank-you card. He included his telephone number, fax number, pager number, and e-mail address. This list certainly seemed very inviting. A few days later, she phoned to tell him she was coming to the city and that she'd like to stop by his apartment to see his computer equipment. She jokingly said she would bring some fast food, but instead she cooked a gourmet dinner and, to be prepared, she took her toothbrush and a package of condoms with her!

That evening she found a very neat apartment (although somewhat later she saw that his bedroom, where the computer equipment was located, was very cluttered) and a table set attractively, complete with wine glasses. There was a fire blazing in the fireplace, and music by Mozart quietly filled the room. Two friendly cats greeted her. Gayle was positively impressed.

After they ate, Jim brought out a deck of tarot cards. Both Jim and Gayle believe that tarot cards can predict the future. Jim's thought was, "Let's see what God set in my lap."

Much to their surprise (and pleasure!) the cards that each selected and played showed fortunes in each other's favor!

"Do you know what this means?" asked Gayle.

"I think so," Jim replied.

"Then why don't you invite me to spend the night?"

"Sounds good to me."

At this point, Jim's thought was, "Is this what I've prayed for—someone special for me?"

EDITH

 Though he might not have been as specific in his prayer as Gayle was to her Goddess, Jim has the strong belief that his entreaty to a higher power helped bring Gayle to him. I believe that many happy couples have the conviction that God helped them find each other.

They had a very good first night together. "The most wonderful ever. He's very knowledgeable about sex," confided Gayle.

The next night Jim phoned Gayle to thank her. Since she had

forgotten to look at his computer the previous evening (did she really forget?), she agreed to return that night . . . and again the next night. Then after a weekend that they spent at her house, she suggested, "How about a permanent relationship?" Jim agreed.

A few weeks later, Gayle told Jim that she had a one-month trip to Mexico planned. Her son was married to a Hispanic woman, and she was going to visit them. Jim agreed to stay in her house to take care of the animals and watch over things while she was gone. At that time, Jim had a regular job as an editor for a magazine, which meant an hour-and-a-half commute to work each day from Gayle's house. But to him, it all seemed worth the effort. A few days after Gayle left, this became questionable when a big storm flooded the road and caused some landslides that made travel treacherous. Yet, he stayed on and persisted in caring for Gayle's home and pets, still getting to work.

When Gayle returned from her trip, they both realized that neither one had enjoyed being apart. So Jim agreed to make a permanent move into Gayle's house. As he settled in, Jim thought he'd like to get married right away. To him marriage meant "a formal legal commitment. With a ten-year age difference, marriage gives us a firm ground of love and commitment together."

Gayle said, "I could live like this the rest of my life, but I know marriage is important since other people see it as a permanent, legitimate relationship."

When they discussed wedding plans, Gayle explained that she would be 60 years old in a few months and until then it would not be practical for her to be married. The reason to wait was in order to qualify for Social Security benefits from her deceased husband's account. The law states that if she were to remarry before age 60, she would lose all payments, but by marrying after 60 she could start to receive payments when she reached 62. With this consideration, they planned the wedding to take place after her sixtieth birthday.

What Were Your Early Years Like?

Gayle

Gayle was the youngest of five children in a poor, struggling family that was native to the area in which she now lives. Her father was a farmer and, on the side, a musician. He was an alcoholic who physically abused her mother. As a child, Gayle was sexually molested by an uncle. Gayle's parents quarreled constantly, and she finally left home at age ten to live with an aunt and to later stay with other families until she could become independent. In many of the homes where she lived, the men attempted to sexually molest her, but she managed to fight them off.

I asked Gayle how she survived such a childhood. "I had an aunt who said I was a 'changeling.' This meant I was really a gypsy child brought into the family. From a very early age, I thought I was an ancient spirit in a child's body so that I could watch what was happening in my family and not be a part of it. In the second grade, I began to read Greek myths and they became part of my fantasy life. Often during the summer, I would retreat to a special private spot under a bridge by a creek near our home. There I could look up at the sky, see the butterflies and shapes of clouds, and hear the bubbling creek beneath. I would commune with my protectors, the Good Fairy and the Greek Goddess Artemis. Another of my protectors was from the comic strip *Wonder Woman*. Wonder Woman's mother was the Goddess Minerva, who lived on Mt. Olympus. With these protectors, I was not a part of the fighting and chaos in my home. Sometimes I drew pictures of these powerful women or made little clay statues of them to keep near my bed."

EDITH

 Gayle is a perfect example of the "transcendent child" as presented by Lillian B. Rubin in her book *The Tran-*

scendent Child (1996, HarperCollins Publishing). This book describes individuals who had horrendous childhoods and not only survived them but, as did Gayle, excelled as adults. Rubin uses the term "disidentification," which literally means "not identifying with." The adults she describes could look clearly at their families' crazy behaviors and not blame themselves or feel unworthy. As a child, Gayle, through her fantasies, did exactly this, creating a narrative that separated her from her family and helped her grow into a happy and successful adult.

Jim

Jim's family was not an affectionate one. His father had an alcohol problem but was able to manage a restaurant and be both a painter and a sculptor. Jim's mother was a secretary for many years. He grew up with one sister.

From an early age, Jim wrote poetry and short stories. His parents were proud of these accomplishments, and he dreamed of being a writer when he grew up. He later graduated from college with a major in English and creative writing. After some difficult years with frequent unemployment, he found work as an editor for a well-known magazine.

What Were Your Previous Relationships Like?

Gayle

At age 14, while a high school sophomore, Gayle met her husband-to-be, who was ten years older. They were married two years later, when she was just 16. Their marriage lasted 38 years.

After marrying and finishing high school, Gayle completed a

two-year course at an art institute, majoring in sculpture. She then stayed home for ten years, raising two daughters, and sculpting in a studio her husband had built for her. When the children were older, she became an assistant manager of a department store. Eventually, she completed a master's degree in business administration. This advanced education led to employment as an administrator in a branch of a large corporation and eventually to opening her own art gallery, thus combining her business expertise with her love of art. She soon became involved in many local community activities and remains so to this day. She also joined the Chamber of Commerce, serving as president for several years. She helped sponsor the girls' soccer league and has volunteered to teach sculpture in the local community center.

Gayle's husband started his career as a technician with an automotive company. He rose to an administrative position, eventually becoming financially well off. They had a good, mutually supportive marriage for 28 years. According to Gayle, her husband always gave her what she wanted materially. But for the last ten years of their marriage, he developed a serious drinking problem. Although he was not abusive while drinking, it nevertheless seriously affected their marriage. Among other things, the drinking made him sexually impotent. During this time, Gayle tried to help him but to no avail.

EDITH

 Impotence is a frequent result of heavy drinking. Trying to "help" an alcoholic never works. The person must recognize his problem and seek treatment himself. I refer spouses or other family members of serious drinkers to Alanon. Here they learn to stop "enabling" behaviors, as well as how to avoid being consumed by their partners' drinking problem and how to take care of themselves within the relationship.

Early in their marriage, Gayle had been deeded the land from her mother that she and Jim now live on. She and her husband decided to build a house on the property. Gayle took charge of the project, planning an energy-efficient house, and getting the construction started. But they never lived together in their new house, because before it was completed, her husband had a fatal heart attack. This was quite a shock to Gayle and, as we spoke, tears came to her eyes. (Her husband's ashes are in a jar on a shelf in the living room.)

Gayle concluded this discussion by saying, "After my husband died, I dated some nice men and, if I had been responsive, I could have married any one of them. But I was not going to settle for less than I really wanted. Also, I really missed having a good sexual relationship." She told me she was not sexually involved with any of those men. A year-and-a-half after her husband died, Gayle met Jim. She strongly believes that her husband's spirit guided Jim to her.

Jim

Jim's sister, while in college, had a roommate whom he met when he was 20 years old. He married her two years later, and the marriage lasted 13 years. They had one child, a son. Throughout the marriage, Jim and his wife had difficulties supporting each other emotionally. His wife wanted him to be like her father, who had an entirely different way of life. She resented being the sole breadwinner during Jim's periods of unemployment. Jim became depressed and "felt isolated, as in a cave."

As time went on, Jim's and his wife's differences increased, and their arguments became more frequent and more bitter. Jim said, "I didn't understand a lot of the things she needed. I was being an ass. If I had the opportunity to do it over again, I wouldn't make the same mistakes."

EDITH

 That Jim could take responsibility for the breakup of his marriage, rather than blame his wife, impressed Gayle. It takes two to tango, and in any failed relationship, it is important to look at your own behavior as well as that of your ex-spouse.

After their divorce, Jim's depression changed to a negative and cynical attitude toward life. Now that he is with Gayle, his cynicism has been replaced with positive emotions.

Before meeting Gayle, Jim had brief affairs with a number of women but nothing serious developed. Before his relationship with Gayle became sexual, he had an AIDS test, which is important for older individuals before becoming sexually active again. (Infection with AIDS is alarmingly high in the over-50 population. See statistics on p. 275.)

What Problems Were Faced and What Adjustments Were Made?

When I asked Gayle and Jim about the problems they encountered in their relationship, their immediate comments were: "I don't believe we've made many changes. On further thought, I suppose we have made some minor adjustments. It's difficult to identify any problems we've had except for little ones like Jim leaving things around the house and not picking them up. I like neatness. We don't have any arguments, but we do have discussions over differences, once in a while."

EDITH

 Quite a few couples I interviewed could recall few, if any, problems and adjustments. As the interviews progressed, however, they eventually remembered difficulties they had experienced and willingly talked about them.

When I raised the question, "How does your age difference affect things between you?" I received the following responses:

Gayle explained, "I was nervous at first. I was concerned about my appearance and what his friends would think. When I prepared for a party at his office, I actually dyed my hair, used new makeup, and wore bright clothes—all to look younger. I also remember one time when we visited a museum and I noticed a woman with a young boy looking at us. I listened carefully and heard her say, 'That must be her son with her.' The young boy replied, 'No mom, that's her boyfriend.' What a perceptive child!"

Then Jim added, "I never feel the age difference when I'm with Gayle. We have come to realize that it actually is more of an issue to people around us than to us. Some people question why we're together. Because Gayle is wealthier than I am, I must have married her for her money. Not true."

"I remember one time," Jim continued, "when we were with some friends, one asked me, 'She's a lot older than you, isn't she?' I replied, 'If *I* were older than *she*, you'd never ask that question.' It's a question that relates to our culture and we should realize it shouldn't be asked or even thought about."

As our talk progressed, Gayle and Jim described ways they relate to each other that makes their relationship so successful.

Gayle commented, "We're very open and honest with each other."

"Yes," replied Jim, "I've told her that if I'm doing something that really offends her to please tell me. I may or may not be able to change but if I don't know then I can't try. I screwed up my first marriage and don't want to do it again. We always try to talk problems over."

When Jim first moved into Gayle's house, she expected him to help out with many of the physical tasks necessary around the house and the grounds. These included repairing fences, cutting wood for the fireplace, pulling weeds, and all the other chores necessary to maintain a large acreage in the country. She also wanted some computer work done quickly for an organization. Jim was confused. He could handle the computer work, but being a "flatlander" (hill people such as Gayle, call valley folk "flatlanders"), he found other tasks daunting. Which should be done first?

When Jim expressed his confusion to Gayle, she had to ask herself, "What's really important *right now*?" She decided, "We can get someone to do the outdoor work so Jim can spend time on what he does best, work on the computer."

Now Jim cuts firewood, pulls weeds, and handles some of the other physical chores that he enjoys, but he spends most of his time on computer projects.

One major problem and consequent adjustment was Gayle's drinking that started in her youth and returned after her husband died. Despite her heavy drinking, she was able to remain functional and continue with her many activities. Gayle did not acknowledge that she had a problem.

One evening she and Jim, whom she encouraged to drink with her, were both quite drunk. They needed to go somewhere in the car and she decided to drive. The result was that she ran into a tree, totaling Jim's car and causing him to suffer five broken ribs. She was arrested and faced serious legal charges. This became the "moment of awakening" for Gayle. She stopped drinking, started counseling, and attended Alcoholics Anonymous. As Gayle said, "That was the time when we started to feel more trust and honesty between us. The experience helped us to see things more accurately and clearly."

Because of her good reputation, continuing extensive community services, and her attendance at Alcoholics Anonymous, Gayle was put on probation rather than given jail time. From then on, with additional support from Jim, she did not drink.

Gayle laughingly changes an AA saying, "God grant me the serenity to accept the people I cannot change, the courage to change the ones I can, and the wisdom to know it's ME."

Jim listened attentively as Gayle described her victory over alcoholism. After awhile he took her hand in his and said, "Before I met Gayle I had a sarcastic outlook on life. I made fun of everything. That attitude has changed as a result of living with her. I have a new way of looking at life. She brings out a more nurturing feeling in me."

At this point, he took her in his arms, and said, "I'm so grateful to you. I feel like I have a chance to be a human being again." Remaining in Jim's arms, Gayle kissed his cheek. "You let me know what makes you happy, and it's often me—just being me. That brings me so much joy."

What Are Your Ongoing Activities?

Gayle continues her work with her gallery, her sculpting, and her many volunteer activities. Jim has tried to slow her down, with little success. Everything she does gives her satisfaction, pleasure, and recognition, all of which are important to her. Jim admits that he enjoys watching Gayle accomplish things while helping other people. He also participates in some volunteer work with her.

Jim left his editing job soon after moving in with Gayle. His freelance editing work has increased, and he is deeply involved in writing a novel. He and Gayle also collaborate on projects. They both brainstorm a problem, consider and select development ideas, and then Jim completes the written work on the computer.

Though occupied with their many activities, Gayle and Jim try to control their time together. Sometimes they take a day off to relax, hang around the house, stay in bed, or go for walks. A lot can be accomplished at home because they do not watch television. Watching films on video and listening to music are good entertainment substitutes for them.

Some Final Thoughts

In their rich and satisfying life together, Gayle and Jim have received what each had prayed for and what Gayle asked for in such detail from her Goddess. They knew what they wanted, and they found it. They have defied the cultural expectation that the man should be older than the woman. May they be an example to many—*vive la différence!*

CHAPTER 8

Building a New Life with an Old Friend

Laura and Ed

"With our first mates, we lived nearby, played golf, and socialized together. Then my husband and Ed's wife each passed away within a year. A divine plan, like a miracle from above, brought the two of us together, leading to our joyful union. We are very fortunate."

From a Long Friendship to Marriage and Advancing Age

Friendship before romance, is one way to build a strong foundation. It enables a couple to learn about each other from a distance, without the expectations of a committed relationship.

Socializing as two couples, Laura and Ed were able to observe each other's interactions with their respective spouses. As their friendship developed after their mates' deaths, they supported each other, sharing thoughts and feelings. The qualities they recognized in each other during this time of grieving stood them in good stead when, after many years of their own marriage, they began to deal with the difficulties of advancing age.

Introducing Laura and Ed

I walked into the elegant lobby of a large retirement facility, rode the elevator up to their floor, and walked down a long hall to the door of Laura and Ed's apartment. Both Laura and Ed greeted me, and we sat at their kitchen table to talk. The apartment was small, sunny, and pleasant. Ed's oil paintings decorated the walls.

"We don't have too much room here," said Laura, "but there is so much to do in this community that we are out a lot of the time. And because most of our meals are provided, we don't need a big kitchen and dining room."

Laura and Ed have been married for 19 years. Laura, age 80, is of average height, with coiffured white hair and smiling hazel eyes. At 90 years of age, Ed is a tall, heavy-set man with a head full of gray hair. Because of an irritated throat, he sounded rather gruff, but I was pleased to find him quite friendly, contributing much information during our interview.

Ed is a retired bank manager. Before her first marriage, Laura was a beautician, and then for many years she was a housewife and mother.

How Did You Meet and How Did Your Relationship Develop?

When Laura and her first husband moved to a retirement community many years ago, they became acquainted with Ed and his wife, who also lived there. This was first through their mutual participation in local sports, which later expanded to include social activities together. The couples became good friends. After several years, Laura's husband died suddenly of a heart attack. Ed's wife passed away from cancer nine months later.

Faced with similar sorrows, Laura and Ed helped and supported each other during their time of grief. At first they were just friends, with no emotional attraction. They saw each other frequently, grieved together, and comforted one another. As their lives settled down, together they went to church, played golf, shared community activities, ate dinners, and attended dances.

When Laura went by herself on an overseas cruise, Ed realized how much he missed her. Laura nodded her head, saying, "I had a feeling for Ed that was more than casual. Being apart told me something. I suppose the expression 'absence makes the heart grow fonder' was very appropriate in this situation."

After Laura returned from the cruise, they became even closer and more affectionate, holding hands and hugging. Their need for each other continued to strengthen. "We were not getting any younger," exclaimed Laura, "so we agreed that marriage was the thing to do."

A year after Ed's loss, they were wed. Laura's daughter, who recalled the beautiful wedding her mother had arranged for her, told Laura, "Now it's my turn to do this for you!"

After his first wife's death, Ed thought it was depressing to continue living in his house with so many memories of her. He sold the house, disposed of most of his possessions, and taking only his desk and leather lounge chair, moved into Laura's house in the retirement community. Laura said, "Staying in my own home was important to me since women like to have their own things."

How Were You Attracted to Each Other?

Laura recognized Ed as a stable, wonderful person. She knew how faithful and dependable he had been to his first wife. Her husband had been reserved and not very affectionate. Ed was very affectionate, very considerate—a positive change for her.

Ed thought Laura was beautiful to look at, always happy and smiling. Now that he lives with her, he says, "She looks like an angel when she's asleep." But Ed soon noticed more than just her physical appearance. He also saw Laura as a caring person. She comforted him when he grieved for his wife, and now she takes care of him as his health fails.

What Were Your Previous Relationships Like?

Ed

Ed met his first wife in high school. They built a close, devoted relationship during their courtship and 45 years of marriage. They had two sons. His wife had been very athletic and participated in many activities with Ed. He showed me some early photos taken with her, admitting that he "still thinks about her now and then."

Ed retired at age 62 and, with his wife, moved to the retirement community where they met Laura and her husband. Two years before their move, his wife developed cancer, and she died after ten years of illness. Ed was then 70 years old. It had been a good marriage, and his wife's long illness and death were painful for him.

Laura

Laura was married to her first husband for more than 39 years. They had a son and a daughter. Her husband was a businessman, giving her everything she wanted materially, but under the surface there were many differences and mistrust. For her, their sexual relationship was not satisfactory, and she felt insecure because she was aware that he "played around" with other women. Looking back, she believes she may have been too dependent on her husband to leave him, because she was afraid she could not make it on her own financially. This is a problem for many women, particularly for those who never worked or had a career. In comparison, she now feels totally accepted and loved by Ed.

"In those days," she said, "women were not so independent, and we didn't talk about difficulties with our husbands. We were committed to our marriages, no matter what. You can't judge our behavior then by today's standards."

Laura's husband retired at age 55, and they moved to the retirement community where they became acquainted with Ed and his wife. Her husband died suddenly from a heart attack when Laura was 60 years old.

What Are Your Present Lives Like?

Laura and Ed left the retirement community where they first met for one where meals, housekeeping, and transportation are provided. Despite the narrowing of their worlds as they age, Laura and Ed lead happy and active lives. Primarily their continued joy is in being together, and in their small apartment they are very much together. Although they have had to give up some of their former activities, such as golf, they still find pleasure in other, less demanding pursuits. They continue to enjoy visiting with their children and grandchildren.

Both Laura and Ed have some health problems. Laura suffers from arthritis in her hands and one knee, and she has an irregular heart rhythm. Until a few years ago, she was an avid weaver, but her hands have lost their flexibility. She has a hearing aid in each ear and treats her hearing problem with humor. "The hearing aid really helps. When Ed is watching something on TV that doesn't interest me, I just turn off my trusty aid and continue reading."

Ed's problems are much more limiting. He has had severe difficulty with his heart. He has had two bypass operations and two blockages removed from his arteries. He takes medication to control angina and thus has curtailed many of his more strenuous activities. This was a gradual slowing down for a man who once was very athletic.

Because of Ed's problems with his circulatory system, he and Laura have become much more careful with their diet, consuming small amounts of red meat, more fat-free and low-cholesterol foods with little salt, and sugar-free desserts.

EDITH

 This dietary practice is slowly becoming more common among older persons as they become aware of habits for good nutrition. It has been proven that by eating more fruits, vegetables, and grains, while reducing fats, sugars, and red meat, health can be improved.

With eating discipline and moderate exercise, many seniors are controlling or even overcoming high blood pressure, heart conditions, potential stroke, and obesity. Those who started these practices earlier in life can see health benefits now, and I believe Ed would be having fewer problems now if he had followed this regime at a younger age.

Fortunately for Ed, Laura is an experienced caretaker. She began as a child by caring for her mother, who had a heart problem, and although she has had no formal training, she has nursed several friends back to health over the years. She believes "Someone" is watching over her to aid her in the ability to heal. She helped herself when she suddenly suffered a serious miscarriage during her first marriage. At that time, she prayed for God's help and then felt a "presence" guiding her back to health.

When talking about this supernatural feeling and her desire to support others, she expressed that she was "not afraid of anything in order to assist people—I just do what I have to do." Ed agrees that Laura exhibits special powers.

EDITH

 Here Laura, perhaps because of her early role of caring for her mother, now feels no resentment in caring for her husband. This is different from **Naomi**, who openly expresses resentment without guilt. We need

> not judge either attitude if it is comfortable for the person concerned.

Until the past few years, Laura and Ed took frequent trips to Hawaii, Europe, and elsewhere. Now traveling is too exhausting for Ed. They used to visit Laura's daughter's cabin in the mountains, but they now find the altitude difficult for their hearts. For the past six years, Laura has accepted the responsibility for all driving, as Ed suffers from macular degeneration, which has affected his eyesight.

Activities in their present retirement community have replaced much of what they have had to give up. They take trips by bus to many interesting local sites such as museums and parks. The residence's bus transports them to stores, the theater, and restaurants. They enjoy social events with the many new friends they have made in their community. Laura volunteers as a tutor in a nearby school, and a few times a week both Laura and Ed play bingo.

For many years, Ed was able to enjoy the community garden plot, growing flowers and vegetables. Until recently, he visited his plot of ground several times a day during the season, but now recognizes his physical limits for this activity. "I really hated giving up my garden," he said, "but life goes on."

Ed was an accomplished artist, and many of his paintings adorn their apartment walls. Now, because of the macular degeneration, he no longer can paint. Giving up so much that he enjoys, first golf, then his artwork, and even his beloved gardening, has caused Ed to suffer from occasional bouts of depression, but he does not allow himself to sink into lethargy. He continues to be as active as possible at home, making the bed, taking out the garbage, and helping Laura with lunches and laundry. As his ability to engage in former activities fades, he still keeps his mind active. Now he enjoys crossword puzzles, using a magnifying glass to aid his failing eyesight.

EDITH

 Depression is common with increasing age, and this is understandable, given the many losses of bodily functions and previous pleasures that people experience. Continuing to be useful at home, as does Ed, bolsters flagging self-esteem and lessens depression. We all face losses as we age, and it is important to keep our bodies as active as health permits and our minds alert.

For the mind, Ed chooses crossword puzzles, even though he must use a magnifying lens. Others might prefer playing bridge or Scrabble, taking courses at a local college, or using a computer. But as much as keeping an active mind or body, it is also important to experience positive emotions. Laura and Ed have the companionship, love, and respect for each other that help keep depression at bay and life, with advancing years, worthwhile.

Some Final Thoughts

A quality of friendship exists in any good relationship, whether the couple has been friends first and sweethearts later or sweethearts from the start. Many happy individuals refer to their mates as their best friends. Not all of our couples had a period of platonic friendship before they became committed. Many became romantically and sexually involved quite quickly and still have successful relationships.

It is important to fully explore issues between you and your prospective partner and then to become truly comfortable and at ease with that person. Would this person you are so attracted to at age 60 be there to care for you at age 80, as Laura cares for Ed? Would he or she be able to face the declining years with courage and dignity, as does Ed? If the answers to these questions are "yes," you and your partner will hopefully live out your years together with grace, kindness, and love.

CHAPTER 9

When Married, We'll Never Be Bored

Edna and Seymour

As Edna and I talked, she told me, "I felt drawn to Seymour when we first met. Our relationship grew over the next eight months. Then Seymour decided to visit his niece in Chicago. When he returned, he told me he had met someone there and had asked her to marry him! By now, I loved him and was devastated. Even so, I still cared enough for him that I wanted him to have what he wanted. Even though he married another woman, I had a strong premonition that he would return to me in time." And he did.

Patience and Accepting the Unexpected

Edna showed great patience and flexibility in accepting Seymour's unexpected marriage. This is not an invitation to accept a bad relationship and put life on hold, waiting for it to improve. Edna had an inner certainty based not merely on the astrological signs she believed in, but on the reality of experiencing a good partnership with Seymour. She had the wisdom to know that men often act rashly after a wife's death and that Seymour's hasty marriage might not last. She had the patience and acceptance to be there for Seymour when he returned to her.

Introducing Edna and Seymour

Edna is 73 years of age and Seymour is 75. Seymour is a retired attorney, and Edna is a retired social worker. From the time of our first interview, they had known each other 16 years, meeting when he was 59 and she was 57. They have been married ten years, living together five years before they wed. They now live in a comfortably furnished condominium in a large retirement community. Edna's landscape photographs adorn the walls, and in the living room is a display of Indian arrowheads from Seymour's collection.

When I went to their home for the interview, Edna greeted me with her morning coffee in hand at 11 a.m. She is a late riser. She wore an iridescent violet jump suit and was limping from a pinched nerve in her leg, incurred while gardening. She has short, auburn hair, a slender build, and was friendly and direct.

Seymour arrived about two hours later, having come directly from a doctor's appointment, dressed casually in shorts and a T-shirt. An attractive man, he has a warm, direct manner, and a magnetic quality about him. Despite his obvious intelligence, Seymour has developed a memory problem with age. Edna had to remind him of their appointment with me, and she keeps track of their busy schedules.

How Did You Meet?

Edna had been divorced for four years before she met Seymour. His wife had died suddenly of pneumonia three months before their meeting. With a lady friend, Edna had attended a number of dances for older singles, and she did not find any men that interested her. She had heard of a club known as Parents Without Partners and thought that through it she might make some contacts for her youngest son, so she attended a club dance.

Edna met Seymour beside the refreshment table. After a brief introductory conversation, she thought he was interesting enough to ask him to dance. After a few steps, they danced closer together, and so their attraction to each other started, leading to a satisfying sexual experience in her home that first night. (By the way, Edna never mentioned whether she found any friends for her son through this club!)

How Were You Attracted to Each Other?

Seymour wanted a partner close to his own age. To him, Edna exhibited a good personality, was outgoing, and pleasant to be with.

EDITH

 It is refreshing to meet a man who explicitly states that he wants a woman close to his age. Many men seem to be looking for, or are involved with, much younger women.

Edna experienced Seymour as outgoing, a good dancer, and a very caring person. Her intuition told her that this man had something about him that was right for her. It is this inner sense of rightness that sustained Edna later in their relationship when Seymour left her to marry the other woman.

How Did Your Relationship Develop?

For the first eight months after their meeting, Edna and Seymour remained in their separate homes but saw each other almost every day. Neither stayed overnight in the other's home, as they both had teenagers living with them. Still, they felt comfortable enough to go into a bedroom, close the door, and have sex.

When he was in Chicago, visiting his niece, Seymour met a lady, believed he was in love, and rashly asked her to marry him. He returned and told Edna, who was surprised and hurt. Seymour sold his house, loaded his personal items into a rental truck, and drove to Chicago. Edna loyally volunteered to drive with him. For a month after he married, they had no contact, but Edna still had faith that Seymour would return to her.

Their relationship should have ended when Seymour married. But as Edna, a believer in astrological forecasts, stated, "From the beginning, our astrological signs and our personalities seemed to match so well, and I strongly felt that, ultimately, we were destined to be together."

EDITH

 It's not unusual for a man who has been married for many years to jump impulsively into an unwise relationship after the death of his spouse. Edna understood this. She also realized that Seymour had had little time to grieve before he met her, just three months after his wife's death, and less than a year before he married the woman in Chicago. As his wife's death was quite sudden, he had no chance to prepare for her passing and to say goodbye. Perhaps moving to Chicago was a way to flee from memories of his wife's death and his grief.

Shortly after his hasty marriage, Seymour realized that it was not working out. He discovered that his wife was an alcoholic, and they had frequent bitter arguments. He had his own brand of patience; he did not want to hurt this women and decided not to leave her until she said that she wanted to end the marriage, which she finally did. Meanwhile, unhappy with his poor choice, he contacted Edna.

Edna told me, "Within a month, on my birthday, I received beautiful roses with a note: 'With love, Seymour'. It was a lovely thought. Shortly thereafter, he started to phone me every Sunday. My tarot cards told me he would return in January. After six months, Seymour divorced his wife, returned in January, and moved into my house." Edna's patience and her belief that she and Seymour were meant to be together were justified at last.

Edna had an exceptional lack of rancor and ability to let Seymour find his own way. After he returned, his daughter said to Edna, "I'm surprised you took him back after what he did to you."

Edna replied, "He didn't do anything to me. Sometimes you have to let go if you want someone to come back to you."

Edna and Seymour lived together for five years before they married. The first four years they lived in Edna's home. The last year, they purchased the retirement-community condominium where they now reside. During this time, Seymour never directly told Edna that he loved her. He called her "darling," and as Edna said, "He showed his affection for me with his eyes. I often noticed tears in his eyes and I assumed that he needed time to grieve for his late wife before committing himself to me. I didn't pressure him. I just waited patiently."

Then one day, while shopping together in a large department store, at the top of a flight of stairs, Seymour paused, looked directly at Edna, and said he loved her, asking, "Will you marry me?" They were married shortly thereafter by a judge, on a date that astrological signs pointed to as propitious.

What Were Your Early Lives Like?

Edna

Edna was the oldest of three sisters. Her parent's marriage was an unhappy one. Her father, an alcoholic, often would spank the children when drunk, but in spite of that, she felt close to him. On the other hand, her mother would force the children to go into a field to cut switches. Then she would beat them with the switches until they stopped screaming. Despite the fact that her mother abused her and her siblings, Edna stayed home, worked, and helped support the family.

EDITH

 Even as a young adult, Edna was patient in seeking love, but her longed-for closeness with her mother never occurred. Fortunately, her patience with Seymour won her a good relationship with a man who truly loves her.

Seymour

Seymour was raised in an orthodox Jewish family. His parents were both immigrants from Europe. He had one sister, five years younger. His father, a doctor, worked as a milkman to support the family during the Depression. Seymour describes his childhood as a happy one. He was especially close to his father, who took him to ball games and movies. His sister married an Israeli, moved to Israel, and still resides there. Seymour feels a strong allegiance to that country and has visited Israel several times with Edna, who is not Jewish.

What Were Your Previous Relationships Like?

Edna

Edna married her first husband when she was 23. During their 25 years of marriage, they had four children—two boys and two girls. Her husband was an insurance agent, and their income was erratic. Edna helped support the family by working on and off in various social work agencies. She and the children received little love or attention from her husband. He had a long extramarital affair, and Edna learned of it one day when the woman called the house. Although her husband broke off this affair, the marriage remained very strained. Edna felt unable to leave because of her concern for their four children. During this time, she became depressed and often thought of killing herself.

Toward the end of her marriage, the whole family went into counseling. The counselor told Edna that her husband wanted a divorce. Sometime after he left home, she learned through a friend that he had had another long-term affair during their marriage.

EDITH

 Edna showed patience by staying with her first husband 25 years despite much unhappiness. In retrospect this might seem unwise, but with four children one does not leave a marriage lightly. Although her husband was the one who asked for the divorce, Edna was strong enough to finally leave him and then make a good life for herself and the children.

The patience that Edna showed later in life with Seymour was of a different genre, and the results are much happier than those of her first marriage. Her sensitive awareness of the positive qualities in Seymour gave her the inner strength to be patient.

Seymour

Seymour was married to his first wife for 37 years. They had three daughters. He had tears in his eyes as he spoke to me of her. His wife died three months before he met Edna. He describes their marriage as a good one, but at the same time he told me she was strong willed, held grudges, and was responsible for a feud among his children that is still ongoing.

Edna believes that it took Seymour five years to finish grieving and ready himself to propose marriage because his feelings for his wife, though deeply loving, were also somewhat ambivalent. Conflicting emotions are harder to accept, and the entire process may take longer to work through on either a conscious or an unconscious level. Seymour, who is not as psychologically sophisticated as Edna, only knows that for five years he had abnormally high blood pressure, which abated after his marriage to Edna.

What Are Your Present Lives Like?

Edna and Seymour see themselves as soul mates and as being mentally in tune. They often know what the other is thinking and feeling. Frequently they have the same thought at the same time and see themselves as mirror images of each other. Their marriage is filled with fun. They laugh, hug, and kiss a lot. A good part of their humor consists of teasing each other. At first, their children thought they were fighting, but now they realize that is just how this couple interacts.

After I finished interviewing Seymour, Edna entered the room. "I've just been telling her what a terrible wife you are," Seymour told her. Edna laughed and rubbed his back.

EDITH

 Humor is an important part of Edna and Seymour's relationship, as it is with many older couples. It buffers conflicts that may arise over habits previously formed. It can also alleviate sadness that comes with declining health.

Edna and Seymour's joy in being together is augmented by their many activities. Edna makes and sells ceramics. Seymour collects and displays Indian arrowheads. Edna is also a photographer and displays her work. They play golf and workout in the community gym. They read and discuss the same books and have traveled extensively.

Edna and Seymour's Advice

Edna and Seymour offered some useful suggestions to other older persons who are forming new relationships. They stress acceptance of one's partner for who he or she is.

They say, "When two people get together, they have to explore their thoughts and feelings. This takes time and honesty. There are always differences, and you have to decide which ones you can accept. Some compromises and adjustments are necessary, but you really cannot expect another person to change his or her essential self. Too many people perceive what they think the other person wants and try to fill that role. You should always continue to be who you are."

Some Final Thoughts

Edna showed unusual acceptance of Seymour's brief, unwise marriage and the time it took to grieve for his deceased wife before being fully committed to her. Seymour was accepting of Edna's beliefs in astrology and psychic phenomena. Their basic compatibility became the most important factor in their relationship.

It's very unusual for older couples, newly coupled, to have the experience of a partner leaving for another and then returning, but all must show patience in accepting differing beliefs and habits. It also takes patience and understanding to wait until your partner is fully committed. Often, after the death of a beloved spouse or a bitter divorce, one partner may take much longer than the other to open his or her heart fully to a new relationship.

Seymour and Edna tell us to first decide what you can live with and what's really important to you. If you then make the choice to be with someone, acceptance of that person as he or she is will be essential to a good relationship.

CHAPTER 10

"Are You Two in Love? I Saw You Hugging."

Karin and John

Karin and John taught Karin's six-year-old granddaughter to ride a bicycle. They were so delighted to see her confidently riding, they embraced each other. The granddaughter asked, "Are you two in love?"

"Yes, why do you ask?" said Karin.

"Because I saw you hugging."

Respecting Different Needs for Closeness

Often the two individuals who make up a couple have different needs for closeness. John would like to live with Karin. She's much more cautious, and he is willing to wait. They recognize and respect these dissimilar needs in each other, and while continuing to live separately, they enjoy a loving relationship.

Introducing Karin and John

Karin's and John's residences are about a 20-minute drive apart. I visited John first. He rents a sparsely furnished apartment in a large city. John is an attractive man and looks much younger than his 69 years. He is tall and well-built, with thinning reddish-gray hair, and piercing blue eyes. He was intense and direct during our interview.

John retired from a career in county social services at the age of 50. He began earning additional income by managing several small businesses, and today he teaches ballroom dancing several evenings a week. He has been twice divorced and has had several other long-term relationships.

Karin lives in a home in a nearby suburban community. Her home is very pleasant, sunny, spacious, and attractively furnished. Karin comes from Denmark. She is 65 years old, but also looks much younger, and is tall, blond, blue-eyed, and speaks with a slight accent. Karin was friendly, frank, and gracious during the interview.

Karin has been a widow for 13 years, and John is the first man she has been involved with since her husband's death. When I saw her, she had been retired for less than two weeks from a job as an office manager that she held for the past seven years. Toward the end of our interview, John came to her home and I saw them there together.

How Did You Meet?

Karin and John were both members of the same ballroom dance club. John was involved with another woman at the time, but often danced with Karin. Each time he danced with her, he would forget her name. "I have a thing about forgetting a woman's name, especially if I'm interested in her and I can't act on it." Karin eventually got annoyed with him and said, "If you don't want to remember my name, forget it." He never forgot her name again.

After about a year, John broke up with his girlfriend, and it took him a year to recover his good spirits. Finally, still attracted to Karin, and knowing that she was a hiker, he invited her to a club's lodge on the coast. Coincidentally, they were both members of the same club. At first, she consented, but then she had second thoughts. "I can't sit in a car with him for two hours. He never talks." So she called him and made an excuse not to go.

Several weekends later she went to the lodge with a girlfriend, and John was there with a friend. All four hiked together and had a great time. "I discovered that when we walk together, he doesn't stop talking!" So began their relationship.

What Attracted You to Each Other?

John expressed many reasons for finding Karin attractive. In fact, he was drawn to her before he was free to act upon it. He liked that she was in good physical condition, with a lot of energy. He recognized that she was down to earth, smiled easily, flirted, and had fun when she danced. He always has been attracted to somewhat different women and liked her Danish accent. "I love to look at her, love to dance with her, and love the way she talks." He was also attracted to her being a grandparent and very devoted to her grandchildren. At first, he was concerned that she was overloaded with obligations, and was perhaps a bit jealous, but now realizes that "it's who she is."

Karin thought she wanted to get to know John, even when he was involved with another woman. She was attracted by his looks, the way he danced, and that he seemed to be a pleasant person. As she knew that "looks can lead to a disappointment," she saw more in John than just a nice body and attractive facial features. Personality is expressed in the way one's body is held and moves. A smile, an expression, or the look in one's eyes, all shine through and give a message.

How Did Your Relationship Develop?

Very soon after the hiking weekend, John asked Karin to a concert and then to three social activities. Thinking he was rushing her, she accepted the concert, but refused the other invitations, using work as her excuse.

John went on a trip for a week, and when he returned, he and Karin became closer and eventually became involved sexually. According to John, "I fell in love pretty fast—but it wasn't like in the past. Formerly, I'd fall in love with no questions. This time I used some judgment and waited for a go-ahead from Karin. I used to think I could change a woman who was rejecting me." Laughing, he continued, "I thought I was so lovable, how could anyone resist me?"

During that summer, Karin went for a long visit to Denmark, and on her return, she and John resumed their relationship. While Karin was still working, they spent weekends together, mostly at her home as it was larger, and they saw each other once or twice during the week for dancing. Since she has retired, John stays longer at her home, approximately four days a week. He keeps some clothes in the closet of her extra bedroom. They are planning a vacation of several weeks, their first vacation together.

What Were Your Early Lives Like?

Karin

Karin was raised in a small, rural town in Denmark. She was the middle child, having an older brother and a younger sister. Her father was an accountant and died when she was 12 years old. She didn't get much affection from either parent but there was stability, and she knew she was loved.

Karin has many happy memories of her childhood. In the winter, she skied to school and skated on frozen ponds. In the summer, she picked berries with her siblings and ate home-grown produce from the family's garden. Karin left home to go to college on a scholarship. She graduated with a degree in languages and also attended business school. After finishing school, she continued to live on her own and worked in business. As an adult, she is able to be affectionate with her mother, who is responsive to it. Her mother, in her 90s, is in failing health in a rest home in Denmark. Karin phones her weekly and visits every year.

John

John was raised in Southern California, the youngest of three children, with an older sister and brother. His father was a lawyer, and during his early childhood, the family was quite well off. When he was seven, his father died. John recalls his father as working long hours, but being warm and affectionate, playing with him and his siblings on weekends. His mother became ill with rheumatic fever after her husband died, and when she recovered, she went to work as a telephone operator. John believes she had the best of intentions, but it was hard raising three children alone and working full-time. There wasn't much time for affection. When they misbehaved, she threatened to send them to a home for wayward children. John described his relationship with his mother as one in which he was always trying to make her happy for fear he might be sent away. John believes this has much to do with his neediness and his desire to please the woman he is with.

On the positive side, John and his siblings were active in scouts, sports, and many other activities. This has continued into his adult life. Even now, at almost 70, he is still active both physically and socially.

What Were Your Previous Relationships Like?

Karin

When Karin was 25, she met her 27-year-old husband-to-be at a summer Quaker youth camp in Denmark. People from all over the world attended, and he was from the United States. She came to this country with him, and they were married here. The marriage lasted 27 years. They had two sons. Her husband was a chiropractor and she helped in his office. He died at age 54 of a lung disease caused by being exposed to asbestos while in the Navy. Karin had a long grieving period, but she was never depressed and was able to function, mainly because she could cry freely.

EDITH

 There is a real difference between grief and depression, and the outward expression of grief does much to dispel depression. I personally know the difference. I was in my forties when my brother died, and at the time I was unable to cry. Outwardly I seemed okay, but for two years it felt as though a pale gray screen stood between me and the world. When my husband died, I was 62 and alone in our home. I was finally able to cry and, yes, scream and howl. My grief was interspersed with periods of being able to enjoy life and so I never felt that gray, grinding depression.

After her husband's death, Karin went back to college and attained another degree, this time in business administration. She enjoyed school, where she had always excelled, and this helped her self-confidence. She obtained an administrative position with a chiropractic society that lasted for seven years, until her retirement. Much like **Naomi**, who also experienced a lengthy first marriage, Karin enjoyed a period of being alone with increasing independence. If she felt lonely, she called a friend and shared activities. Unlike Naomi, she did not date, but neither woman engaged in sexual activity until their present relationships.

EDITH

 For women like Karin or Naomi, who were in lengthy, traditional marriages, widowhood brings a new experience of working and being in charge of their own lives. No longer answerable to husbands or children, once the initial grief is past, their new freedom is exhilarating. No wonder Karin has been reluctant to give this up in exchange for the closeness of living with John.

I asked Karin if she noticed similarities between her deceased husband and John. "Yes, they are both a little quirky. That's the kind of person I like. Danes are very straight-laced, and I like unusual people." John, like her late husband, doesn't enjoy shopping for clothes; he does like to play jokes, and he is not overly concerned with money. Her husband grew a beard, biked to work, and did a lot of pro-bono service, so they never became wealthy. Thus, it doesn't bother her that John lives in a simple manner. "Though," she stated, "I wouldn't move into his place—it's too small."

EDITH

 Like **Gayle**, Karin is not concerned that her partner is less well off financially than herself, and should they eventually live together, John would share her house as **Jim** shares Gayle's home. It was easy for Jim to move in with Gayle, and John is not disturbed at the thought of leaving his small apartment. In fact, he already partially lives in Karin's home.

Karin feels free to talk to John about her husband and tells him some funny incidents from her marriage. John, in turn, has no difficulties talking to Karin about his previous relationships.

John

John married his first wife when he was 25 years old. The marriage lasted 20 years. They raised three boys and a girl. During this time, John worked as a county social worker. When the children became teenagers, his wife began to have difficulties with the children and engaged in severe arguments with the eldest. Rather than fight, John remained outwardly the model husband, but distanced himself emotionally from his wife and family. "I had worked myself into a hole, playing the role of a good husband and father, and neglected to take care of myself. I felt I had to get out from under these burdens," he disclosed. "I had dreams that I would curl up and die if I didn't leave." He and his wife went unsuccessfully to family and couples' therapy. Then John attended a ten-week personal enrichment encounter group (such groups were common in the 70s). "At the sessions, I had a taste of what it would be like to leave the marriage. I felt more life and energy." At age 44, John divorced his wife. He continued to see his children regularly and always paid child support. He is now a committed grandparent.

After his divorce, John had a number of relationships. His second marriage lasted 11 years. His second wife was better off financially than he was, so he moved into her house and worked in her business. After a number of years, she began to take trips without him, and he felt lonely and rejected. After several separations, they finally divorced.

Following his second marriage, John had another relationship in which he lived with a woman for five years, but with whom he had many conflicts. "It was a mess, and I should have ended it much sooner."

John was involved in another fairly long relationship in which they did not live together. The lady was 12 years younger and had teenage boys. It did not work out. And, as might be expected of an attractive, socially active man, John had a number of other romances of shorter duration, one with the woman with whom he was associated when he first met Karin at the dance club.

EDITH

 John's ease in finding women substantiates the belief that it is easier for an older man to find a partner than it is for an older woman to do so. But finding a partner isn't enough. John's previous relationships did not work out well. It needs to be the right partner, and you need to be ready emotionally. (See Chapter 23 for information about being ready to find a partner.)

Because John obviously was hoping that he and Karin would go on together indefinitely, I asked him in what way this relationship differed from others in the past. He said that he sees Karin as a much more secure and settled person than the other women in his life. The exception was his first wife, a stable woman, with whom he lived for 20 years, but unlike his first marriage, with Karin there are no problems of work or raising children. Also, more than in any other previous relationship, he and Karin are able to talk out their differences so that he is not left holding resentments.

To Live or Not to Live Together…
That Is the Question

Though Karin and John reside separately, they started talking about living together early in their relationship. The understanding is that John will eventually move into Karin's larger, more comfortable home. It is John who is eager for them to live together. "I feel better, more secure, when I'm living with someone," he said. At the same time, John is aware that he tends to be "emotionally needy" and is in psychotherapy to deal with this issue. As much as he wants to live with Karin, he doesn't want to rush into such an arrangement, as he did previously. Karin is hesitant and is in no hurry. Neither of them has made any mention of marriage. Karin is afraid that living together would take away some of the romance between them. She likes not seeing John for a day or two and then looking forward to being with him.

Karin wants living together to be on a trial basis so that if it doesn't work out, John would not have lost his very desirable apartment. Karin is nervous about both of them being retired, having unstructured time on their hands, and thus getting on each other's nerves if they live together. She also is concerned about this extra time when living alone, and plans to take courses and serve as a volunteer.

EDITH

 Unstructured time often is a concern as an individual is about to retire. I went through a brief period of anxiety prior to my retirement from the agency where I had worked for many years. However, it did not take me long to structure my time; in fact, it became too full. I find this true of many active retirees and many of the couples interviewed.

What Are Your Activities and Interests?

Karin and John have many interests in common. They dance, walk, and bike together. John also runs regularly. They both love classical music, enjoy going to the movies together (they have the same taste), and like discussing the film afterwards. John takes tai chi at a senior center and, now that she is retired, Karin plans to join him.

One thing that they definitely do not share is John's love of spectator sports. He watches sporting events a great deal on television and reads the sports section of the newspaper. If he reads details aloud to Karin, she tells him, "I'm not listening." Karin told me, "It's ironic—I've ended up with the same type of person as I had before. My husband loved horses. He rode, went to the races, and read about bets, odds, and race payoffs. I was never interested." With John this difference is no problem. Karin sometimes knits or reads while she watches a game with John, or she just goes to another room and does something else.

What Adjustments Have You Made?

Karin has a very positive outlook on this issue. "John is flexible . . . very easy to be around. It's amazing, there are no adjustments. We just seem to flow. He helps with chores when asked. I'm a neatnick, but he's neat too." They both like the same food, near to vegetarianism, and often cook together. "He eats faster than I do, but my husband did too," she added, "I just ask him to slow down. It doesn't really bother me."

John tends to be self-critical and is concerned that he is four-and-a-half years older than Karin. He believes he has always had a poor memory, especially for names and places, and that it is getting worse now that he is older. He thinks that sometimes this annoys Karin. Also, because of being older, he worries that he naps during the day more than Karin does. John is tired after running or after many hours of dancing, and I believe he is just beginning to accept the fact that perhaps he can't do as much physically as formerly without some extra rest. He is pleased that Karin has started to need naps too. Of course, it is good to keep physically active when older, but it is also necessary to accept with grace whatever natural slowing down occurs with age.

Some Final Thoughts

For Karin and John, the question as to when, if ever, they will live together is still unsettled. John's desire to live with Karin comes from early insecurities. He is aware of this issue and is working on it in psychotherapy. Karin, after a long marriage in which she was a housewife, is reluctant to give up her newly found independence and is much more cautious about their living together.

These differing needs for closeness occur frequently in older couples in the early stages of a relationship. If both partners understand and respect each other's desires, there should be minimal conflict over whether or not to live together. Decisions about the future can be put aside, and then each partner can, as do Karin and John, entirely enjoy their full and happy new life together.

CHAPTER 11

Trouble...Trouble... Will It Last?

Joyce and Bill

They started off with high hopes, with similar values and interests, first becoming good friends and then living together. After a year, things gradually deteriorated. "Now we seem to be just biding our time to see what's going to happen between us."

Are Common Interests Enough?

Despite many difficulties, Joyce and Bill are still together. They have a multitude of common interests: they both enjoy hiking and camping, fine dining, and reading similar books. Bill's grandchildren are important to both of them. But is all this enough to make up for the power struggle in their daily lives and the resulting lack of tenderness and sexuality in their relationship?

Introducing Joyce and Bill

Joyce is 64 years old, soft spoken, with brown hair and eyes that easily tear when discussing her relationship with Bill. Bill is 66, with a trim build, a gray mustache, and an outgoing, friendly manner. He is gregarious and talkative. She is a bit shy and more of a listener. They met three years ago and each is retired.

They live in Joyce's house in a small, rural community. Joyce does a lot of crocheting and knitting; she enjoys gardening and continues with her artwork. The house is reasonably neat but cluttered, containing many antiques and some valuable paintings that Bill brought with him. They have two pets: Bill's dog and Joyce's cat.

Joyce has a degree in art. For 30 years she was a teacher and still is active with her freelance art projects. Bill is a retired fireman and is now skilled at using a computer.

How Did You Meet?

Both Joyce and Bill belonged to the same hiking club. The club meets in the mountains near Joyce's home, and she hiked with them regularly. Bill lived in a nearby city, and he joined them occasionally. On one outing, Joyce and Bill walked together and engaged in an animated conversation. They lunched together after the hike, and the attraction between them began to grow. As Bill said, "Our meeting took place at the right time for both of us."

How Were You Attracted to Each Other?

Shortly after they met, both Joyce and Bill recognized that they liked to do the same sorts of things. Bill admired Joyce's youthfulness, her high level of physical activity, and her artistic nature. Joyce liked Bill's friendly, outgoing personality and was particularly attracted to his grandchildren, as she has none of her own.

How Did Your Relationship Develop?

After hiking and dining together a few times, Joyce and Bill's relationship developed rapidly. Bill visited with Joyce in her home, and she drove to his house, some thirty miles away. After four months, they became sexually involved, and soon after decided to live together in Joyce's country home. They have resided there for the past two years. Bill sold his home in the city, as he was ready for a change and was happy to live in the country.

Early in their relationship, Joyce and Bill considered marriage, but as time passed, they decided it was not appropriate for them. For the first year together, they were both still working, and their life together was pleasant enough. Once they both retired, however, and their time together increased, things began to deteriorate. Without work or children to raise, togetherness can be overwhelming for older people who are newly coupled. Individuals need to have a judicious combination of time together and time apart, which will vary for each couple.

Joyce believed that Bill had difficulties adjusting to what she wanted in terms of housekeeping and daily routines. Bill still felt a strong attachment to his deceased wife, whom he believed understood him and knew how to deal with him, which Joyce did not. He felt controlled by Joyce and wanted more time to himself. These differences resulted in quarrels, followed by long periods of withdrawal.

What Were Your Previous Relationships Like?

Joyce

Joyce had been married twice before, with her first marriage at age 21. They had two boys, but her husband was not close to them, and Joyce had the primary responsibility of raising the children. Her husband earned a comfortable income, but as Joyce said, "Money does not count if you don't get along together." They were divorced after 12 years. Her children are now grown, but she has no grandchildren.

Joyce married again when she was 45 years old. This marriage also lasted for 12 years. Her second husband had a number of extramarital affairs, so Joyce decided to terminate the marriage. At the time she made a vow "not to get married again, but just hang in there and pursue my own life." She was alone and independent for seven years before she met Bill.

Bill

Bill met his wife when he was 17 years old, and they were married when he was 28. The marriage lasted 38 years until his wife died of a sudden heart attack. There were tears in Bill's eyes when he spoke of her. In our discussion, he admitted that he has a hot temper and can be difficult at times. Bill said with fond remembrance, "My wife knew how to handle me."

EDITH

 I wonder how she did "handle" him. Was she submissive? Did she just calmly ignore his temper? This "handling" seems to be difficult for Joyce.

Bill and his wife had two daughters, and now he has three grandchildren. After the death of his wife, one of his daughters, her husband, and their son, moved into Bill's house with him. His daughter became very possessive of the house. This was one of the factors that motivated Bill to sell the house and put some distance between himself and his children.

This daughter's relationship with Joyce is not very good, perhaps because of her jealous attachment to her father. Another daughter's 12-year-old daughter is very close to Joyce, and Joyce very much enjoys having the child visit them. Joyce is an artist, skilled in crafts and handwork, and devotes much time to teaching this young girl. I saw Bill's grandchild when I visited, and she was busily knitting a scarf.

Differences Leading to Problems

Bill and Joyce's relationship is not developing in the manner that either of them had hoped it would when they first became interested in each other. Their discussions with me were very frank. They each clearly revealed the problems they face.

Bill has not emotionally separated himself from his wife. Many others interviewed held fond memories of their deceased spouses but were able to form new attachments. Bill seems to idealize his late wife, speaking of her often in the present tense, although she had been dead for several years. This keeps him from fully committing to Joyce.

In the seven years that Joyce had been living alone, she became self-sufficient, living her life and arranging her home in ways that pleased her. This independence presents a problem for Bill, who sees Joyce as attempting to control him. Also, living in Joyce's house has been difficult, as it has meant fitting into another person's lifestyle.

Unfortunately, Joyce has had little practice in clearly stating what she wants in a manner that is not disturbing to Bill. When she is angry, she withdraws her affection, which hurts and confuses Bill.

EDITH

 To give Joyce credit, with the hurt and anger that Bill feels now, I don't know if he could actually hear her words and recognize her needs. It is not possible to listen clearly when emotionally upset.

Problems with health have added to this couple's difficulties. Joyce had knee surgery a few years ago and therefore hikes on easier trails. This disturbs Bill, who wants her company and urges her to join him on more strenuous outings.

Bill can be irritable because of high blood pressure that is not adequately controlled. He has attended stress-management courses and is now a vegetarian, but his blood pressure medication affects his sexual desire and performance. When their sexual activity first started, it was very satisfying and enjoyable for both of them. Bill helped Joyce relax and become more sexually active, but their relationship problems and the effects of Bill's medication has made intercourse problematic and not very satisfactory for either of them. As Joyce stated, "I feel it necessary to be deeply in love to have sexual fulfillment. Our present relationship does not support good sex."

EDITH

 Concerning a couple's sex life, it is a question of which comes first, "the chicken or the egg." If you are angry and hurt, sex usually is not satisfactory, but the good feelings from enjoyable sex make differences seem much less important.

Financial arrangements are not a problem. Bill and Joyce deposit an equal amount of money from their monthly retirement incomes into a joint checking account to pay for food, house expenses, and taxes. Each one also has a separate account to cover other costs. Being somewhat traditional about money, Bill insists on paying the full amount for travel, dining out, and other entertainment.

Both Joyce and Bill have established separate Living Trusts for each one's assets to go to their own children. However, Bill is considering putting aside a small percentage of his investments for Joyce if he should die first. In spite of their differences, Joyce and Bill handle their expenses cooperatively, and the fact that Bill wants to help Joyce with her future financial security shows his care and concern for her.

What Are Your Thoughts About Your Relationship?

During their separate interviews, Joyce and Bill both stated the same two desires: wanting a close friend and not wanting to live alone. They expressed their positions from both negative and positive viewpoints that indicate the difficulties they face and their ambivalence.

Negative Comments from Joyce:

"I have had lots of arguments in my life, and I don't mean to argue now. When he gets mad and starts to lecture me, I retreat by leaving the room."

E D I T H

 The difficulty is she doesn't return to face the issue with Bill at a calmer time. So their problems fester and get worse with time.

Joyce: "We did not realize our differences then. Things were much better before living together. Now it's like a marriage."

E D I T H

 Because her experience with previous marriages was poor, Joyce thinks marriage is a step down.

Joyce: "He likes to control people, and if he doesn't get his way, he's upset. I won't let him dominate me."

E D I T H

 Bill in turn, feels that Joyce tries to dominate him. They are in a battle for control, as are many couples with problems.

Joyce: "I would like him to be more affectionate."

E D I T H

 He might like affection also. Sometimes it helps to give affection first when you want it from your partner, but you must feel good about the other person to do so.

Joyce: "I am resigned to a relationship of convenience for both of us that is not passionate or sexual. He says he's trapped, but he can leave any time he wants to."

E D I T H

 Does she really want him to leave? Bill has said she'd have to throw him out, and if she wanted to, she could.

Negative Comments from Bill:

"I do not want to be owned or dominated. I need an escape hatch . . . I could take my dog and camp in the wilderness. But if I do, it may automatically be taken that I've given up and am walking out."

E D I T H

 When people feel insecure about each other's feelings, it is very difficult to be honest without being misinterpreted. A temporary need for space sounds like a permanent need to be gone.

Bill: "I'm not comfortable talking with Joyce about my deceased wife."

EDITH

 The degree to which Bill still cares for and idealizes his former wife might be difficult for Joyce to hear, contributing to her belief that he is incapable of making a deep, permanent commitment to her.

Bill: "It seems that the more familiar we get with each other, the worse it gets between us. There are some rough edges in our relationship with some things being taken the wrong way and I don't know how to solve it."

EDITH

 Although it sounds as though they are losing respect for each other, this remark does indicate a desire to make things better.

Bill: "At times it's not worth the effort to be affectionate, and I know she thrives on affection. I don't know what the solution is but I like her and I like it here. I don't want to leave unless she throws me out."

EDITH

 Here he wants her to take the responsibility for ending their relationship.

Among their negative statements are some positive ones that show potential for holding this relationship together and starting the all-important healing process.

Positive Comments from Joyce:

"I know he really tries to be good."

"Down the road we'll get back together."

"We should not break up, it will be too hard on the grand-children."

EDITH

 This is an interesting twist on the reason younger couples use to stay together ... for the sake of their children rather than grandchildren.

Joyce: "When we have problems, we should sit down and talk—map out our goals and decide together what to do to overcome the problem."

"We need to have understandings and make compromises."

"I don't think arguments are settled when people argue hot and heavy. It's a waste of energy. Life is too short."

"I want a loving relationship for the rest of my life."

Positive Comments from Bill:

"Neither one of us wants to live alone."

"I am pleased when she is happy with herself."

"She's so talented and I love to see her artwork."

"We could live together as good friends and companions."

EDITH

 Just "friends"? What about affection and sex?

Bill: "I really think enough of her to contribute to her financial security."

"I want someone to talk to and be playful with."

"I hope a good relationship between us can last forever."

"We should enjoy what we have, and sometimes we do!"

E D I T H

 I particularly like the last statement. Couples with problems often fail to notice the times when they do get along well. Here Bill acknowledges that sometimes they do enjoy each other. Perhaps it is more often than either of them is aware of. I often give couples whom I am counseling an assignment to write down the good times and they are often surprised.

Postscript

I recently contacted Joyce and Bill and was delighted to learn that, though there are still difficulties, their time together is now more pleasant. Joyce has been very supportive and persistent in helping Bill find a physician who is able to prescribe the proper medication for his high blood pressure. His blood pressure is now under control, and he is much less irritable. Joyce in turn is more understanding, as she realizes that there was a tangible, physiological reason for Bill's crankiness. Many of the problems described in this chapter still exist, but Joyce and Bill have an increased respect for the role that medical conditions play in the quality of their day-to-day interactions.

Some Final Thoughts

I see Joyce and Bill as two good people, who are both in pain. The good news in the postscript has increased my hope for the success of their relationship. Are their troubles over? Probably not. Skills are needed in communication and problem solving. They need to learn to listen to each other, not to store old hurts, and to express openly what they do appreciate. Gradually, there will be more space for positive experiences filled with sharing, fun, affection, and enhanced sexuality.

To their credit, Joyce and Bill certainly have hung together through hard times. Neither ever seriously considered ending their relationship, and they never separated, even after a heated argument and a consequent period of withdrawal. This shows a genuine commitment to each other. Perhaps they eventually will be able to look back on these first few years together, knowing that by working on both their physiological and interpersonal problems, despite much *trouble...trouble...their union is lasting*.

CHAPTER 12

It Was Meant to Be

Mary and Fred

Imagine being young and single. You are at a party and find yourself attracted to someone who is married and not available. Then, 35 years later, you meet that same person again and know "this is it." That happened to Fred, who now has been happily married to Mary for more than 20 years. Here is their story.

Reigniting the Spark

Theories abound concerning the chemistry that draws people together. Mary and Fred are living proof that a spark can be reignited even after many years without contact. Given the right circumstances and just a little luck, this chemistry can lead to a lasting relationship.

Introducing Mary and Fred

Mary is 85 and Fred is 79. They became reacquainted 23 years ago. At the time of their interview, they had been married for 22 years. Like **Gayle** and **Jim**, Mary is older than the Fred. Fred is retired from a career in the Navy, where he served as a commander, and Mary spent the majority of her years as a housewife.

They greeted me warmly at the door of their small apartment, located in an elegant congregate living residence. Here, lunch and dinner are provided, as well as housekeeping, transportation, and a large variety of activities. The three of us sat together around the kitchen table. Mary was the more talkative, while Fred made comments in a quiet, reflective manner. He is of medium build, with slightly thinning gray hair. Mary is short, with soft silver hair, sparkling brown eyes, and a lively smile. She is slightly heavy because, as she confided, "You can easily gain weight here."

EDITH

 It is understandable that a costly retirement facility would serve meals with several courses, including attractive desserts. While dietary requirements and preferences are accommodated, many delicious dishes tempt the residents. Most older folks who cook for themselves would not eat the quantity of food provided in this setting. With aging, metabolism slows down, and people are more sedentary. Under such circumstances, a great deal of self-control is needed to avoid weight gain.

How Did You Meet?

In 1940, at a social gathering held by his best friend, Fred met a young woman. At the time, his mind was on completing his college degree and then entering military service. Although she was married, she impressed Fred as someone he would like to see again.

Thirty-five years later, Fred attended the eightieth birthday party for the father of another friend. Again, he was introduced to a lady and had the feeling he had met her sometime previously. "Who was she?" he asked himself. Suddenly it came to him—this was the same person, now a widow, who had long ago so impressed him. "Oh, this is great!" Fred thought.

Mary remembered the two incidents in similar ways. When she met Fred the second time, she felt, "This is it!"

EDITH

 Two of the other couples interviewed, **Ruth** and **Paul**, and **Barbara** and **Leonard**, knew each other in work situations, felt an attraction to each other, but didn't act on it because one or both were already married. Years later they met again and that same attraction was still there.

How Were You Attracted to Each Other?

Fred never forgot his first memory of Mary. At their second meeting, Fred felt good "vibes." Mary offered an attractive appearance and was a good conversationalist.

When Mary met Fred for the second time, she saw him as good-looking and nicely dressed. After being a widow for seven years, she had the feeling that good fortune was smiling upon her.

EDITH

 Neither Mary nor Fred was particularly articulate about what attracted each to the other. There must have been more than good looks and interesting conversation. Fred's statement about vibes makes the most sense to me: an unconscious attraction that neither fully understood.

How Did Your Relationship Develop?

Their next meeting at the birthday party took place near Mary's residence. Fred lived a day's driving distance away. One week later, he phoned Mary to express his interest in her. They corresponded and spoke to each other twice a week on the telephone. A short while later, Fred traveled to see her. Then Mary visited his home, and their relationship grew.

Mary thought she might be considered "old-fashioned," as her moral code decreed "no living together before marriage." Both she and Fred wanted to get to know each other better, so they waited until eight months after their second meeting to marry.

What Were Your Previous Relationships Like?

Mary

Mary was first married when she was 16 years old to a carpenter. Her marriage was a good one that lasted 40 years. She has one son and three grandchildren. Mary cashiered in a department store for seven years, but stayed at home after the birth of her son to be a homemaker and raise her child. Her husband died suddenly of a heart attack, and Mary was then a widow for seven years before meeting Fred.

Fred

Fred is now in his third marriage. The first one, during the war, was very unsatisfactory. That wife was a nurse who just suddenly disappeared. They had one son, who was raised by Fred's mother.

Fred married again after the war. His second wife died of cancer 17 years later. They had no children, but Fred now has a grandchild and two great grandchildren from his one son. Both Mary's and Fred's sons and their children accept their marriage.

What Are Your Present Living Arrangements Like?

When Mary and Fred were first married, they decided to live in Fred's large house, which sat on an acre of land with a magnificent view of the ocean. Mary left behind her son and many friends.

They lived in Fred's house for ten years, but it took Mary some time to feel comfortable in her surroundings.

Eventually they sold Fred's house and moved into a nearby condominium, where they lived for ten years. Then, two-and-a-half years ago, they decided to move back to the area where Mary had lived previously and purchased their present residence in the congregate living facility.

"These moves haven't been easy for me," said Mary. "I'm a people person, and I like to have good, close friends, but I'm a little shy. It took me some years to have a circle of friends and then, just when I felt at home, we moved. I like it where we are now, and I hope we stay put."

EDITH

 Where to live is an important decision for many older couples. When one person moves into the partner's home, that individual will have the majority of adjustments to make—leaving friends, getting used to new surroundings and a new community, adjusting to the partner's standards and expectations in the home, and often parting with many of his or her own furnishings and other possessions. The homeowner also needs to make accommodations to the habits and desires of the new partner.

What Problems Were Faced and What Adjustments Were Made?

Even after 22 years of marriage, Mary and Fred are still adjusting to each other, as are most couples throughout the course of their relationship. They are able to laugh at their disagreements.

"I'm a neatnick," said Fred, "and I'm always picking up after Mary and putting things in their right place."

She made a face at him. "And," said Mary, as she put her arm on Fred's shoulder, "during a bingo game, this man will shout out as loud as can be, 'Be quiet and pay attention.' It's embarrassing." Fred believes that this behavior is a carry-over from his military experiences and might also be necessary because many older folks are hard of hearing.

Fred is on numerous mailing lists and, as a result, receives large quantities of advertisements, circulars, and other types of junk mail. He spends a great amount of time sitting and carefully reading all this mail. This behavior angers Mary, who tells him he is very foolish and should stop it. In return, Fred gets annoyed, pays no attention to her, and usually goes ahead with his reading. Mary concludes, "This is a common practice of men, and I don't fight it." Fred would tell you that if she really wasn't trying to fight it, she wouldn't say anything at all and just leave him alone with his mail!

Mary believes that her first husband, and now Fred, have been over-protective of her. Her first husband did not want her to work outside their home. Now Fred watches her drinking of hard liquor, stating that he doesn't want her to imbibe more than she should. "And I only take one or two drinks a week. He shouldn't be concerned," interjects Mary. At times, Mary wants some privacy and freedom from doing things together with Fred.

EDITH

 Actually, the retirement community offers many activities that Mary could attend without her husband, but the attitude of the times in which she was raised makes this difficult for her. Women of her generation enjoyed little in the way of independence compared with those of subsequent generations. Although the opportunities are there for her, the habits of a lifetime are hard to overcome.

What Are Your Present Activities?

Mary and Fred enjoy many activities together, most of which are provided by their community association. A bus takes them shopping, to restaurants, and to the movies. This really suits Mary, who never learned to drive. They take classes in history and the Bible and attend an exercise class together. They also enjoy taking tours once or twice a year to other countries. "We really do have fun together," said Fred, "and we'll keep traveling as long as we're physically able."

Some Final Thoughts

It is inspiring to know that a spark between two young people can be reignited after so many years and that it can lead to such a happy marriage. As Mary says, "If you trust your own intuition and the chemistry's right, it doesn't matter how old you are—just do it."

Mary and Fred agree that marriage can be more of a struggle when young. In a later marriage, being more secure financially and with their children raised, a couple can have fewer worries and can concentrate on enjoying their lives together. For them, the coincidence of their meeting twice, twice being attracted to each other, and the second time both being free to form a relationship, proves for them beyond a doubt that "*it was meant to be*."

CHAPTER 13

An Unusual Relationship: Married and Living Separately

Carol and Ron

Carol: "We are cosmically connected...drawn together by the forces."

Ron: "And we stuck together ... even through the worst of times. Even when we separated, our commitment was unbroken."

Opposites often attract but it can be difficult for them to live together. Yet while facing one challenge after another, there remains a strong bond of love and support between Carol and Ron. Though their lifestyles and beliefs may differ from those of some readers, their problems and struggles are similar to many that older couples encounter.

A Third Option

Most couples having the amount of conflict that Carol and Ron experienced when they lived together would have ended their relationship. Others would choose to remain living together, no matter how difficult. Carol and Ron exemplify a third option. They are a loyal and loving married couple who live next door to each other.

Introducing Carol and Ron

Carol led me through her home to the deck where we held the interview. Carol is 64 and a retired insurance broker, tall and slim. She was casually dressed in a sweatshirt and pants and during much of the interview, she sat with legs crossed and her feet tucked under her in a lotus position. Her home, which overlooks a lovely garden, felt quiet and serene. Carol's abstract paintings adorn the walls, and in her bedroom is a small altar she uses for meditation. Her cat sat curled at her feet while we talked.

The following day, I visited Ron, age 82. He is somewhat shorter than Carol, with a youthful-appearing, trim body. Ron was an aeronautical engineer, who is retired from his own consulting business. His house is a short distance from Carol's. It is very open, with large windows that let in lots of light. The house is filled with plants, and I noticed a statue of Buddha in the living room. Outside are two birdbaths and a large flagstone patio under a spreading oak tree.

How Did You Meet?

Both Carol and Ron enjoy mountain hiking and camping. When Carol was 47 and Ron was 65, they were participants in a summer pack trip in the high Sierras. The custom for the trip was that as it neared its end, the group would celebrate with a champagne party. That afternoon a heavy rainstorm hit the camp and continued into the night. However, this did not stop the champagne from flowing. The rain flooded Carol's tent, so when it was time for bed after the party, Carol knew she'd never get to sleep in her soggy sleeping bag.

Carol is a feminist with strongly liberal political opinions. Although she saw Ron as somewhat of an "opinionated redneck," she desperately needed to be dry and warm that night. Ron was alone in a nearby tent, and seeing her predicament, he invited her into his dry sleeping bag. Since her clothes were wet, she removed them and joined him. Thus they spent the night together, keeping each other warm, but both insist that there was no sexual activity between them.

During the night, Carol reached over, pulling a blanket over Ron. Ron observed that, "this thoughtful gesture turned the tide for me." Then in the morning, Ron brought fresh hot coffee to her. In turn, for Carol, "This shifted my feelings for him. Juices started flowing."

EDITH

 From the very start, they each expressed a loving consideration for each other, and it was this nurturing quality that each so much appreciated throughout their relationship.

They spent much of the next day together, joking and chasing each other like kids. Carol summarized her feelings for Ron, "I was in love with him—absolutely gone—emotionally deep."

How Were You Attracted to Each Other?

Carol had a difficult childhood without a father. When she met Ron, she saw him as a strong, take-charge, caring person. Although Carol was and still is very strong-willed, Ron must have triggered her need for a father figure. She remembers feeling at the time, "Daddy will take care of everything."

Ron said, "I was fascinated by her. She was different from any woman I've ever met. She was totally uninhibited in her actions. This intrigued me. Falling in love with her was so refreshing."

How Did Your Relationship Develop?

After the end of the camping trip, in spite of the feelings they had for each other, they didn't plan to meet again soon. But a short time later, Carol had severe back pain and, recalling how helpful Ron had been to her in the mountains, she phoned him, asking him to bring a pain medication. He promised to come to her home.

Although Ron was still married to his first wife at the time, they had been separated for two years and their divorce was almost final. It was during this visit that their sexual activity began, and they frequently visited back and forth on weekends. As Carol said, "I have not looked at another man since. We became blissfully inseparable with lots of love between us."

They skied, hiked, motorcycled, and traveled together. Remembering these times, Ron said of Carol, "She was such an energetic, alive person who liked exploring new things and taking chances. I found her so stimulating to be with."

Five years into their relationship, Ron approached Carol in a serious manner, saying "I think we should get married." At the time, Carol saw no reason to marry, but Ron felt "that a marriage license was the only way to protect her financially." Because Ron was more financially secure and wanted to take care of Carol, she finally said "yes."

They chose to marry after spending ten days at a silent retreat in a meditation ashram. When the silence ended, all the participants gathered in a large circle. Carol spoke first to Ron, "You had ten days to think, and I'm wondering if you've changed your mind about our wedding tomorrow."

Ron said nothing for a long, long time and everyone held their breath. Finally, he simply said, "You couldn't keep me from it." They were married the next day at the ashram.

What Problems Were Faced and What Adjustments Were Made?

Eight years after their marriage, they sold their respective houses, and bought a home together, where they lived for five years. At first everything went well between them, but then things began to change. As Carol expressed it, "It became difficult for us to live together. We had one challenge after another. I learned that Ron is extremely compulsive and goal oriented. He is *not* a negotiator. Do it *his* way or not at all! He is used to doing things for himself, without asking or telling anyone. He'd put my things away because he is very neat, and then I couldn't find them. It was extremely difficult for both of us. But when my painful back problem arose, he was very kind and supportive by shopping, cooking, and doing the laundry. But we still argued and had terrible verbal battles. We would yell and scream, and call each other names."

"While there was still a strong attachment between us," Carol continued, "we had to get away from each other. We were not addressing our differences head-on. I bought a home on the coast, and we each started psychotherapy to try to work out our problems. I sold my insurance business, and Ron began to live with me. But he didn't like the people in the town; he thought it was full of hippies and could not accept living there. He was truly miserable. After eight months I asked him to leave, and we began to live separately."

Ron agreed with all of Carol's reasons for their separation and added, "We both had habits that were difficult to give up. She's fussy and more orderly that I am."

EDITH

 It is interesting that both Carol and Ron describe each other as overly orderly, and that they both see this as a problem. People can be orderly in different areas of their lives, which can put a strain on compatibility with a spouse.

Despite their difficulties living together, Carol and Ron continued their close relationship. Ron rented an apartment in a nearby city and often talked with Carol on the telephone. They would get together about three times a month. They still had strong affectionate feelings for each other.

For the next five years, Ron and Carol bought and sold several houses, some nearer or farther from each other, but didn't try to live together again. They talked at length about their differences and the pain each one had caused the other, and while they forgave each other, their disagreements continued. Yet their commitment to each other is unfailing. Today they each own a home in the same subdivision, living just a few steps away from each other.

What Have Your Early Lives Been Like?

Carol

Carol's mother died shortly after Carol was born. Her father abandoned her, leaving her to be raised by his parents. Her grandparents lived on a farm in the Midwest where she was often alone, roaming the fields by herself. Her grandmother was very strict and controlling, and Carol was strong-willed even as a child. Despite her grandmother's whippings, Carol took up smoking and drinking. Her drinking became quite serious and continued even through the early part of her marriage to Ron. (Ron and Carol do not drink alcoholic beverages at all now.) Despite her problem with alcohol, Carol was successful in the work world, first as a secretary and bookkeeper, and then in the insurance business.

Ron

Ron was raised as an only child on a Texas ranch. After his father died, he was brought up by his mother to be independent and self-sufficient. He worked all through high school and, at age 12, he learned to fly an airplane. As a young man, Ron completed a college degree in aeronautical engineering. Before World War II, he worked for a defense contractor but left for military service, where he was trained as a bomber pilot, and later flew combat missions. After the war, he established his own successful consulting practice, which he sold shortly before meeting Carol.

What Were Your Previous Relationships Like?

Carol

When she was 16, Carol got married, mainly to get out of the rural Midwest that she found so suffocating. Her husband was a hardworking man. At that time, Carol wanted to go back and finish high school, but he did not want her to return to school. Carol became resentful at being controlled as she had been by her grandmother. She left her husband, and shortly thereafter they divorced.

A year later, she married again. This marriage lasted for six years but also ended in divorce.

When Carol was 28, she married for a third time. This husband decided to pursue a college degree while Carol worked long hours in an office. The two had little time together and her drinking continued. After seven years, they too were divorced.

Considering her former marriages, Carol sincerely told me, "I could just walk away from them with no problem, but with Ron it's different. I'm totally committed to him and now, at his age, would never leave him."

Ron

During the war, when Ron was 22, he married and had a daughter. He and his wife had little in common and divorced when Ron was in his mid-thirties. Then, three years later, they remarried for the sake of their daughter. They stayed together for 28 years, but as Ron stated, "It became a dead marriage." They divorced shortly after Ron met Carol.

What Are Your Present Lives Like?

In the early years of Carol and Ron's relationship, they "partied" and drank a great deal. "But our health problems led us to turn our lives around," said Ron.

"I had a terribly painful problem with my back," continued Carol. "My spinal discs were degenerating. I was told I would eventually be crippled and be unable to walk. At times Ron even had to help me dress."

Ron stated, "I developed cancer of the prostate about the time we married. I did have an orchiectomy (removal of the testosterone-forming glands that spread the cancer), but in addition to regular medical treatments, we wanted to do all we could on our own to overcome our physical problems."

"So," added Carol, "we went together to a yoga-based, vegetarian-oriented cancer retreat center."

"And that started our journey," continued Ron. "We are still on it, and our health has improved markedly."

Ron and Carol now are vegetarians and grow their own vegetables and fruits in their respective gardens. Together they attend many retreats where they fast and meditate. Carol has studied to become a yoga instructor, teaches a class locally, and gives Ron yoga instruction every Saturday. Remarkably, as the result of their alternative healing activities, Carol no longer suffers with severe back problems. She is able to be physically active and takes daily four-mile walks. Sometimes Ron walks with her, and she slows her pace to accommodate him.

Since Ron is now over 80, they recognize the need to view life from a different perspective than when he was in his sixties. In those days, despite the chronological age difference of 18 years, Ron seemed younger than Carol, both physically and mentally.

Carol recalled several times when she was asked for her senior ID, but Ron wasn't because he seemed so young! But today, they agree that he has definitely slowed down. At first, this was hard on them both, but Ron has accepted that Carol wants to travel and visit friends, and do some things without him.

EDITH

 When a younger woman marries a much older man, as Carol did, she needs to look to the future and know that, at a later date, she might have a much less active companion. If she has her own activities and interests, and her partner accepts them, the adjustment will be much less difficult.

The difference in Carol's and Ron's activity levels can be seen in their daily routines. Ron wakes up slowly and takes a lengthy hot bath. Carol has a special morning time for yoga and meditation. She commented, "Having my own house gives me the psychic and physical space to take care of myself."

They eat breakfast separately, each in his or her own home. After breakfast, Ron goes to Carol's house for his morning hugs and kisses and for a discussion of their plans for the day.

"If I don't see Ron by 10 a.m. I begin to worry," said Carol.

Then during the day, each is busy with his or her own activities. Keeping up two houses and gardens is a lot of work. Carol takes classes, has recently earned her bachelor's degree, and is studying for a master's in alternative health care. Ron likes to shop and to have tea in his favorite café. Dinner together is by invitation. Carol has no television, but she and Ron sometimes watch TV together in his home, often with their arms and legs intertwined as they sit on his couch, hugging and kissing. Sometimes Carol spends the night with Ron, as he has the larger bed.

Ron is very romantic. Some years ago, when visiting a travel agent, he learned of a full-moon kayak trip. "It sounds very romantic," he told the agent. "I'd like to take my sweetie on one of those." And he did just that on Carol's birthday, under a full October moon.

Carol and Ron have a unique way of celebrating each other's birthdays. They start a month in advance, giving each other daily cards or gifts. "A gift could be doing the dishes for a week or giving the other a massage. Any crazy thing," said Carol, laughing.

Sunday is a special time. They both dress up and go to church together, often enjoying an elegant brunch afterwards.

Carol and Ron used to travel together a great deal, but now Ron is mostly a homebody. Carol considers herself a "road warrior," taking off alone in her car, visiting friends, or just going to sit alone in the desert and meditate.

Some Final Thoughts

Despite conflicts and separations, Carol and Ron's love has held constant. Ron loves Carol unconditionally and shows it with daily affection. Carol recognizes Ron's basic trustworthiness and integrity. She states, "If a person has these qualities, other behaviors can be adjusted to, and believe me, we've adjusted plenty." Their primary adjustment has been to live separately, and thus not be compelled to change habits and behaviors each considers essential.

Most important, they have always nurtured each other. Remember what originally sparked Carol and Ron's love? It was her covering him with a blanket that first cold, rainy night, and his bringing her coffee in the morning. No matter what, Carol and Ron are still always there for each other. For them, the commitment of being married and the freedom of living separately is a successful third option.

CHAPTER 14

The Loving Is Easy, but the Living Is Hard

Janice and Cliff

With great feeling, Cliff recites:

How can I tell you of my love?
Strong as an eagle.
Soft as a dove.
Patient as a pine tree that stands in the sun
    and whispers to the wind.
You are the one.

Janice glows as she listens to these words that have so much meaning for them both. Cliff saw the poem while on their honeymoon; he memorized it and had it framed. It is now on display in their house.

Developing Rules for Managing Conflict

Cliff and Janice have diametrically opposed styles of conflict. She's explosive, and he's uncomfortable with confrontation. From their deep commitment and love for each other comes their desire to adapt to each other's styles and, as a couple, they are developing their own rules for managing conflict.

Introducing Janice and Cliff

I was greeted by both Janice and Cliff, given a brief tour of their home, and was then ushered into the dining room, where we held our joint interview. Janice, a recently retired child psychologist, is 55, of medium height and build, with lively brown eyes and a warm smile.

Cliff, who is 67, is a retired physical therapist. He is tall and slender, has gray hair, a gray beard, and warm brown eyes with smile wrinkles around them.

They live in a house with a lovely view of rolling hills from the living area and master bedroom. The furniture is highly polished antique French provincial. A table in the living room is covered with framed photographs of Cliff's and Janice's families from early life through their marriage eight years ago. The house, owned by Janice, has been their home for five years.

How Did You Meet?

Janice had been single for 12 years after a divorce. She knew exactly the characteristics she wanted in a man: intelligent, educated, financially independent, and physically active.

Janice had placed an advertisement in the personals column of the local newspaper, with unencouraging results. Then one evening she went to a singles-club dance, and there she met Cliff.

Cliff was also divorced and had been single six years. During that time, he had been active in various singles groups and had heard the viewpoints of other divorced persons. This helped him consider what went wrong in his past relationships and what he wanted in a woman.

That evening at the dance, Cliff stood at his customary spot by the wall until he asked a lady to dance. When the music stopped, he went back to his spot, but Janice was standing there.

Cliff said, "You're standing at my place."

Janice replied, "I can stand here also. There's room for two."

They started a conversation and then danced together. As Janice exclaimed, "And it never stopped. We danced every dance together that evening. Then Cliff walked me to my car. I gave him my phone number and drove home. It took about 15 minutes to get home, and as I opened the door, the phone started to ring! That was the beginning, and we've been together ever since."

How Were You Attracted to Each Other?

Cliff said, "I immediately liked her conversational manner and wit. She sparkled, showing a lot of life. I was attracted to her looks, her face, and the way her hair was done. I really liked the care with which she put on her makeup and how she dresses in color-coordinated clothes. I appreciated her solid attitude about family and home. Janice is a different type of person than any woman I have known. She lets me know where she's coming from. She seems happy most of the time."

For Janice, "Cliff was a good dancer and I liked that. I was also pleased with the neat way he was dressed and his athletic, trim figure. His conversation while dancing when we first met impressed me favorably. He talked about the sadness of children growing up in poverty. He pointed out the shortsightedness of some social programs in not giving attention to after-school care, nutrition, and family stability. These matters were important to me as a psychologist."

How Did Your Relationship Develop?

Their first meeting at the dance was just before Thanksgiving. Cliff invited Janice to his home to join him and some of his friends for dessert on Thanksgiving Day. She later asked him to accompany her to a friend's wedding reception. So they started inviting each other to various activities in which each one was involved.

Janice continued, "I started to go to his house for dinner, and afterwards we would sit together by the fire. We loved to go dancing a couple of times a week. Our dating became very easy. We both saw our relationship from the first as something different and special. We certainly were attracted to each other."

A few weeks after Thanksgiving, Cliff helped Janice decorate her Christmas tree. She told him that she was planning to visit her family in Massachusetts, and Cliff asked if he could go with her.

"That was pretty fast. I'd known him less than a month," Janice said. "While single, I never had anyone visit my family at Christmas, but I did want to be with him and let my family meet him." She arranged the visit, and Cliff accompanied her. He met all of her relatives and they had a wonderful time.

"We took our time about sex," observed Janice. "We didn't jump into bed immediately, but we did kiss and neck. Actually, we slept together a couple of times in each other's houses—*without sex*. It was three weeks before we had sexual intercourse."

EDITH

 Some couples interviewed would think that three weeks is a short time. Others had sex the night they met. The length of time a couple waits before having sexual relations, including those who wait until after marriage, depends upon their own value system.

Janice continued, "Since we both had been sexually active in recent months, each of us had a blood test that showed no presence of communicable diseases, including AIDS. As a further precaution, Cliff used a condom when our sex started."

Ten months after meeting, Cliff gave up his apartment and moved into Janice's house.

To Cliff, "It felt like a ready-made arrangement—like home. Her elegant furniture and its arrangement in the rooms pleased me. We felt comfortable and stable together."

Janice agreed, "From the beginning, our relationship was not just trying it out. It was real."

Janice and Cliff lived together for a year and then decided to plan a traditional wedding. It took place at Janice's house, with fifty guests in attendance. These included both of their families and close friends. Following the ceremony, they took a cross-country honeymoon in their motor home. When Janice and Cliff were asked, "Why was marriage important?" Cliff's reply was, "That's the way of telling the world I truly love the person I live with."

Janice followed with, "Marriage is a total commitment and that's important to me."

Two years after their marriage, Janice, who is financially more comfortable than Cliff, decided to purchase the house where they now live. Since retiring from her position at the clinic, she has set up an office in the house where she sees a small number of private clients.

What Were Your Early Lives Like?

Janice

Janice was raised in a working-class Italian family on the East Coast. She has only a younger brother. Both her parents were hard-working, spirited people. Despite a lot of arguing, it was a close and loving family to whom Janice is very attached. Both parents are still alive, and she stays in contact, visiting with them and other family members as often as she can.

Cliff

Cliff grew up on a farm as the second youngest of fourteen children! The whole family worked on the farm, and the children were happy, although their upbringing was strict and church-going was enforced. He is still close to his brothers and his one living sister.

Janice and Cliff try to spend holiday times with both his and her families, usually alternating visits on both sides of the country.

What Were Your Previous Relationships Like?

Janice

At age 22, Janice started to live with a man who became her husband four years later. He was a salesman and developed an alcohol problem that, in time, became intolerable for Janice. They were together for 12 years and then divorced. They had no children, which she always regretted. Her husband had a daughter from a previous marriage, who now has three children. Janice was close to these grandchildren during their upbringing and still is. She sees them three or four times a year and plans to provide for their education.

Following the divorce, Janice was single for twelve years, during which time she completed her Ph.D. degree in psychology and became an employee in various public health clinics. She was also involved with a married man for eight years before meeting Cliff. Janice viewed that relationship at the time as "convenient, comfortable, and with few demands."

Cliff

Cliff was married at age 22 while in the service. He had two sons and now has six grandchildren. After the war, he became an insurance agent, but obtained a degree leading to a license as a physical therapist, which was his profession for twenty-five years.

Cliff's marriage lasted 16 years, until his wife initiated the divorce. She gained custody of their two children, which was very disturbing to Cliff. Now Cliff's sons and their children are very close to both him and Janice.

Cliff was single for six years, at which point he married again. In Cliff's words, "My new wife was brilliant but showed no common sense. She would insult people and not even realize it. I don't know why I married her. It was a mistake." This marriage lasted seven years, and then Cliff had several relationships from a few months to more than a year in duration. He broke each one off, feeling it was not right for him.

As the result of his two divorces and his other involvements, Cliff became depressed. He received psychotherapy, attended a divorce support group, and read extensively about developing a good relationship and maintaining a successful marriage. Eventually he became socially active again in singles groups, which finally led him to Janice. As Cliff thinks back, "Those women I knew were very different from Janice. She has a happiness and the ability to express positive emotions not found in my two previous marriages."

What Problems Were Faced and What Adjustments Were Made?

Both Cliff and Janice agree that an individual's family background and upbringing can have important influences on behaviors in later life. Janice, being the first-born child, is well organized and doesn't rest until she has completed everything necessary. She believes she has a "critical parent" inside her and needs to control it.

On the other hand, Cliff, as the second youngest of such a big family has a more laissez-faire attitude. Janice says, "He has a natural exuberance and enjoyment for whatever he does. Wouldn't it be nice to be that carefree? I wish I could be more easygoing. Cliff tells me that he'd like to be more organized."

Cliff builds on this, "She's more serious about life than I am and takes more responsibilities."

Cliff and Janice's deep love for each other is a strong motivation for changing behaviors that cause the other pain. Despite their closeness, they do have difficulties. Here are some of their observations.

Janice

"Small things bother me. He doesn't always close cabinet doors or put down the toilet seat cover. When I see such things not done right, my brain reacts and usually my mouth follows. I feel there's one right way to do things; therefore, I zero in on things not done properly. But I do appreciate things that he has done, like making breakfast for us. When I comment on his mistakes, it doesn't mean I don't appreciate the good things he's accomplished."

EDITH

 But does she openly express her appreciation? It is so easy to notice and comment upon a fault. We so often neglect to acknowledge what our partner has done right.

"I get mad about things more quickly than he does, and I'm louder about my feelings—probably because this is how my family behaved. I know that sometimes I'm just too uptight about small things that really don't matter. I need him to help me loosen up. For instance, when I am critical of his driving, he doesn't like it. When we argue back and forth and raise our voices, we sometimes even call each other names. This often happens when I'm tired, hungry, or cold. But these confrontations don't go on long, because Cliff usually shouts, 'Stop it! Stop it! That's enough.' Shortly after the episode, we always both apologize to each other."

EDITH

 Calling names can lead to deep hurts. It's good that Cliff shouts, "Stop it." It would be best if Cliff and Janice could separate earlier when angry and get back together when calm. Janice could recognize when she is tired, hungry, or cold and thus more likely to explode. Perhaps she could take care of herself in some way (meditation, a short nap, warm clothes, some food, or a hot drink) before taking up an issue with Cliff. After separating until calm, each could decide whether the issue is important enough to discuss at all.

Cliff

"I know I'm not as organized as is Janice and she's super serious and responsible. While I am often grateful for these traits in her, they do cause some difficulties between us. When we do have disagreements, I feel vulnerable because I'm not used to having loud, confrontational arguments. But I realize that her more spontaneous, outgoing style has helped me to recognize my inner emotional self, which is an important gift as you grow older. You can be a bitter old man or a happy old man, and I am more and more a happy old man."

EDITH

 As discussed in Chapter 18, good partners often have the same degree of emotional maturity but are of opposite personality types. Thus, they complement each other and help each other modify their more extreme behaviors.

Recognizing differences of style is a first step in modifying behavior. Janice is trying to react less explosively to Cliff's habits, and Cliff is gradually learning to be more assertive and to both receive and express anger.

What Are Your On-going Lives Like?

Janice observed, "Cliff and I each have lives outside of our relationship. We both have other interests and take time for ourselves. We don't always have to be together every minute. I like to read and watch old movies on television, write letters, or edit my professional newsletter. Cliff has become active in many community organizations in this area and he also spends a lot of time in our garden. Then, when we are together, it's even more special."

Janice and Cliff used to travel a good deal, but now, since they both have physical difficulties, they travel less. They frequently go out to dinner and spend evenings playing cards and watching television: Janice prefers light entertainment, while Cliff goes for historical programs. Because they have two TVs, they occasionally watch separate programs. Sometimes they rent a video to enjoy an old movie together. Cliff likes to read novels and nonfiction history, while Janice still reads her professional literature in addition to popular fiction and nonfiction.

Until a few months ago, Janice had a cat as a house pet, but it has since died. Now they are preparing to acquire a dog for companionship.

EDITH

 Pets can be an integral part of an older couple's family, almost like a child. The benefits of having a pet, particularly for older people, are well documented.

> Sharing the responsibilities for a pet, receiving and giving affection, and the interaction are all extremely good for both physical and mental well-being.

Some Final Thoughts

Some conflict is inevitable in any relationship. Cliff realizes this when he says "Marriage is made in heaven—so are thunder and lightning. We must live with it all."

Many couples come from different family backgrounds with different styles of conflict. This often is an advantage. If both partners are explosive, chaos can result. If both are very controlled, disagreements may never be dealt with, which can lead to growing resentment and eventual disengagement. Each couple needs to form their own explicit or implicit rules for managing conflict. Then each partner needs to modify his or her own behavior in accordance with these rules.

It isn't easy to be in an intimate relationship with another human being. It takes the love and commitment that Cliff and Janice so amply possess and the realization that, as so aptly expressed by Cliff, "*The loving is easy ... it's the living that's hard.*"

CHAPTER 15

An Ideal Older Relationship: *It's a Smoothie!*

Barbara and Leonard

"When I first met him, Leonard was good-looking—WOW!—and he still is! We felt a lot of chemistry between us, but we knew it was not going anywhere."

"I've been a flirt all my life, and Barbara responded in the same way. I certainly wasn't straying from my loyalty to my wife; this was casual fun between us."

That was more than 20 years ago. Now they are a happily married couple with an ideal relationship.

A Connection that Transcends Time

Have you ever had a special friendship with a person of the opposite sex where you knew on some deep level that you had found someone you could trust and love? Barbara and Leonard formed such a friendship through their profession and, at the time, it was combined with a sexual attraction they were not free to act upon. After many years of no contact and then a lucky, brief meeting, Leonard communicated with Barbara, and they reestablished their relationship.

Such reconnections occur fairly frequently among older adults. If you are single and longing for a partner, think back and try to locate a person with whom you had a bond. There is always a chance that person may be available again. And, if you reach out, you might also find that you and your friend have a connection that transcends time, as Leonard and Barbara did.

Introducing Barbara and Leonard

It took me some searching to find Barbara and Leonard's rural home, and I arrived a bit late for our interview. Both greeted me warmly and ushered me into a home that had been designed and charmingly decorated by Barbara.

Barbara is 64, and Leonard is 70. They are both retired probation officers and, at the time of our interview, had been married for just a year. Barbara is tiny, with short, straight gray hair and smiling hazel eyes. Leonard is more than six feet tall, and slim, with a handsome, square face and blue eyes. Both had a confident manner and were very frank and open as we talked. They expressed a great deal of affection throughout the interview by looking into each other's eyes, blushing while they spoke, and frequently touching each other.

How Did You Meet?

Barbara and Leonard served in probation departments in the same county but in different divisions: he in adult, she in juvenile. During fairly frequent social gatherings, they became acquainted, chatting and dancing together, and sharing job experiences.

At that time, Barbara was engaged and Leonard was married. As Barbara confided, "We felt a lot of chemistry between us, but we knew it was not going anywhere."

How Were You Attracted to Each Other?

Barbara

"Sometimes you meet someone and shortly thereafter you feel like you've known that person forever. There was that kind of rapport between us right from the beginning. We talked easily together, probably because we were in the same occupation. And our thoughts flowed together so smoothly."

Leonard

"I liked her smile. She had a warm way of communicating and relating to me. She had a well-built body and she danced well. Her attitude about her work was very positive, and I admired that."

How Did Your Relationship Develop?

After a number of years, Leonard transferred to another county. Fifteen years later, they encountered each other at an RV dealership. They recognized each other, had coffee together, and visited.

By that time, Barbara was divorced. Leonard, who had retired a few years previously, told her that his wife was ill with cancer. Because Barbara had suffered from breast cancer herself, she understood what Leonard was going through and sympathized with him.

When Leonard's wife died a few years later, he found that he wanted to talk with Barbara. "She'll understand," he thought. Four months after his wife's death, Leonard found her phone number and called her. She invited him to her house for lunch.

EDITH

 As the result of a long-term study of happily married couples, Robert Levenson (a psychologist at the University of California) states, "I would argue that knowing how a person reacts when a partner expresses sadness is the most valuable piece of information to have if you're concerned about having a happy and lasting relationship." (*East Bay EXPRESS*, Berkeley, CA, July 9, 1999, page 9.)

Although Levenson doesn't use the words *compassion* and *understanding*, I believe that those are the reactions that need to be displayed when a partner expresses sadness. Barbara was able to do this, and Leonard was perceptive enough to recognize her ability to empathize with his pain. He sensed that she would be there for him as he grieved for his wife. This empathy between them was part of their original connection, and Leonard, in actively seeking out Barbara, reestablished their tie.

When Leonard arrived at her house, Barbara recalled, "He looked like a whipped puppy." Obviously, he was miserable to have lost his wife to cancer after their 49 years of marriage. Yet neither could help noticing that there were still sparks between them.

Leonard remembers, "Things between us heated up fast." Leonard drove the fifty miles to Barbara's rural house, where they now live. After three visits, he said to Barbara, "It's a long ride home for me. Can I stay overnight?"

"Sure," Barbara replied.

"Where can I sleep?" was the next question.

"Wherever you want to," came the response.

"That was it!" They both nodded and laughed together.

They soon settled into a weekly visiting pattern, but soon even this wasn't enough for either of them. Barbara had been enjoying her single life after her divorce, but "I did want him around, and I wasn't prudish about sexual matters. It didn't take long for me to hate it when he drove out of my driveway after a visit."

During his earlier married years, Leonard had felt that if anything should happen to take his wife, he would prefer to live with a woman but not get married. "But when the time actually came," Leonard stated, "this idea didn't seem right." While they both wanted to be together, it did not feel proper to live together without being married. They particularly didn't want to give the wrong impression to family and friends, especially coming so soon after the death of Leonard's wife. They became engaged and, when Leonard had first visited Barbara, he fell in love with her house in the hills, so they easily made the decision to live there.

When they look back at those times, they realize that Leonard never actually proposed marriage. They just understood it was what they both most wanted in order to bring them completely together. A simple, non-denominational wedding took place in May in the garden of Barbara's house. Leonard's son was the best man and Barbara's daughter was maid of honor. Family and close friends attended.

What Were Your Previous Relationships Like?

Barbara

Barbara was married for the first time at 20. This marriage lasted for five years, during which time she had two girls. She supported her husband for much of the time, as he did not work regularly. He became physically and verbally abusive, and she eventually divorced him.

Her second marriage was to a man twenty-two years her senior. While amicable, the marriage was not satisfactory, because they were so different in their likes and dislikes. It ended after four years.

Barbara was then single for seven years. At age 38, she married again. This husband served as a father figure for her two girls, but he was a drinker and became abusive. It was during this time that she developed cancer. Barbara said of her husband: "He was good to me during my illness, but as I recovered, my attitude toward myself changed. Until then, I'd been a slave to my family. I realized that I had to take care of myself and I became more assertive in terms of my own needs. I've learned that it's physically harmful to internalize anger. I decided I was going to beat this cancer and I gave my husband an ultimatum—either quit drinking or give me a legal separation." He left, and after ten years, they divorced.

EDITH

 In Barbara's case, knowing that she had to take care of herself led to leaving a marriage in which her needs were not considered. This radical change in her life's outlook, I believe, led to her choosing Leonard—someone who fulfills her needs and brings her happiness.

When I asked Barbara to compare Leonard with her previous husbands, she made this observation: "There is no comparison. He's the gentlest man I've ever met. He's loving, sentimental, and so good. He's like a big teddy bear."

Leonard

At age 20, Leonard wedded his 18-year-old high school sweetheart. It was a good marriage that lasted 49 years, with two children, a boy and a girl. From the time when the first symptoms of his wife's cancer were detected, she lived five-and-a-half more years. Leonard took care of her until the end.

As Leonard described his feelings, "A year ago, I couldn't have talked about her without crying. It still gets me a little bit. I turned to Barbara for comfort, and she has helped me so much." Barbara put her arms around Leonard and stroked his back as he spoke. She continues to have the ability to empathize with his sadness, showing no jealousy of his former wife. This is an important part of their strong connection.

In addition to Barbara's comforting presence, living in her home has given Leonard a fresh start and has helped him recover from his grief. Both his wife and his mother died in the house where he had lived for many years, and it held many sad memories for him.

What Are Your Ongoing Activities and Interests Like?

Leonard and Barbara's closeness is strengthened by the many activities they enjoy together, such as gardening, reading, and taking long walks.

They both participate in various community services. Before meeting Barbara, Leonard had traveled little outside of his job requirements. Barbara, on the other hand, had taken many trips. Now they are traveling together and are planning their first ocean cruise to Hawaii.

Together they are also taking a seminar about writing memoirs. Leonard was somewhat reluctant at first, but with Barbara's encouragement, he is now enjoying the class.

EDITH

 Memoirs are an excellent way of finding a sense of continuity in life and sharing this life with children, grandchildren, and perhaps even great grandchildren. When a couple writes the history of their lives together, they are also sharing their personal stories with each other. This cannot help but add to their sense of closeness.

Some Final Thoughts

What is the basis of the strong connection between Leonard and Barbara? When they first knew each other, they formed a genuine friendship, based partially on their common experience as probation officers. This mutual understanding of past experiences enriches their present happy marriage.

When Leonard and Barbara first met, they felt a strong sexual charge between them. Because she was engaged and he was married, they had enough loyalty to their respective partners not to act upon this attraction. This restraint cannot help but have increased their respect for each other. Respect and an awareness of each other's basic integrity in both their professional and private lives were instrumental in their reconnecting more than two decades years later.

Because Leonard and Barbara had been good friends in the past, Leonard knew that Barbara was compassionate enough to help him with his grief. It might have been luck when they met again at an RV dealer's showroom, but Leonard deliberately sought Barbara out when his wife was dying, and she continued to support him during his grieving.

Acceptance of a partner's sadness is a very important element in all relationships. Friendship, sexual attraction, basic integrity, and compassion are all factors in this connection that has transcended time and has led to an ideal older relationship.

PART TWO:

Important Topics for
Older Couples

CHAPTER 16

Relations with Adult Children and Grandchildren

Interactions with adult children are a very important aspect of almost every new, older couple's relationship. A study by the Gerontological Society of America gives evidence that a close, affectionate tie between adult children and their parents (or a parent) can contribute significantly to prolonging the parents' lives. Most of our interviewees found acceptance of their new relationships by their children, but some, unfortunately, did not.

Adult children might have difficulty accepting their parent's new partner for various reasons. They may be very attached to the deceased or divorced parent and think it is disloyal for their mother or father to find a new love. They might be unwilling to share their parent's love or attention with another. Or, they might fear that they will lose part of their inheritance.

Often adult children have difficulty conceiving of their parents as sexual beings. It is not too different from young children who, when they learn the facts of life, find it hard to believe that their parents actually "do it." When I was a child, my grandmother remarried at a late age. My parents were glad that she had found a companion, but it was clear that they did not believe she could be sexual.

When Jerry and I got together, my daughter knew we were sexually involved but definitely did not want to know any details. "After all, you are my mother," she said emphatically. Certain boundaries need to be kept between parent and child, even an adult child. My daughter accepts Jerry. She is an adult, so in no way is he a step-parent to her. She treasures her father's memory and she also enjoys Jerry's friendship and company. She is pleased that he makes me so happy.

The following are some examples of both positive and negative interactions with children and grandchildren:

Ruth and Paul

Paul's wife, although still alive when he first became involved with Ruth, was suffering from Alzheimer's disease, and was completely incapacitated and uncommunicative. To marry Ruth, he had to divorce his first wife, while continuing to provide financial support for her as long as she lived. Paul talked with each of his three children, pointing out the many years he still had before him and expressing his desire to be free to have a better life with another woman. His children fully supported him. Ruth also wrote to Paul's children, telling them, "In no way would I take your mother's place. Your father and I will just be companions to each other for the rest of our lives."

All their children, Paul's three and Ruth's daughter, attended their wedding and have happily accepted their new relationship. It was good that both Ruth and Paul communicated with Paul's children before divorcing their mother to marry Ruth. Of course, they themselves were aware of their mother's decline with the disease, their father's care for her, and his lonely life when she became fully incapacitated.

Karin and John

Karin resides separately from her partner, John. She has two sons, one of whom lives at a distance. He and his wife have met John briefly and have accepted his relationship with Karin. Another son and his wife live nearby. They have a girl and a boy, and Karin baby-sits for them regularly. John has spent several nights at their home when Karin was baby-sitting, and the grandchildren have visited in Karin's house. The grandchildren are very fond of John. Recently, the three-year-old said, "I love ma-ma (grandma), and I love John too." When the grandchildren visit in Karin's home, they ask, "Where's John?"

John's four children have all met Karin and like her. John still spends holidays and birthdays with his ex-wife and adult children, which gives the children a connection with their past. Surprisingly, Karin accepts this situation with equanimity. Perhaps the fact that she lives separately from John makes this easier for her, although she might feel differently should they live together or marry sometime in the future.

Joanne and Andy

Joanne and Andy have a similar situation. They are not married but are living together. Andy's daughter resides nearby with her mother and visits often. She very much likes and admires Joanne, who had been helping her prepare for job interviews. However, her mother did not invite Joanne to the daughter's college graduation. This made Joanne extremely angry and hurt, though she realized that her lack of status as a "wife" and the relative newness of her relationship with Andy, were probably contributing factors.

One of two things needs to occur to change this situation that was so hurtful to Joanne. Either she could gradually come to accept not being included in his daughter's celebrations, or Andy could confront his former wife on Joanne's behalf, even to the point of refusing to attend an occasion himself unless Joanne was included.

Although their situations were similar, Karin's and Joanne's reactions were different. I can only surmise the reasons for this difference. For one, Joanne lives with Andy, while **Karin** and **John** reside separately. Also, Joanne has a much more volatile personality than does Karin. There is no right or wrong reaction for not being included in an occasion involving your partner's children. Situations will differ and the uniqueness of each individual needs to be recognized when attempting to resolve such a problem.

Barbara and Leonard

Leonard, who is married to Barbara, has a son and a daughter, and eight grandchildren. Barbara has two daughters and two grandchildren. Both discussed the plans for their marriage with children and grandchildren. One of Barbara's daughters, and all of Leonard's family, accepted and anticipated the event with pleasure. While Barbara is close to her one nearby daughter, it's Leonard's children and grandchildren who primarily make up their family.

When Leonard was first courting Barbara, his teenage granddaughter often took care of his dogs. After a few times, she became curious, asking him, "Where are you going, grandpa? Are you seeing someone?" He answered by asking, "What would you say if I told you I am?" His granddaughter replied, "I'd think it was wonderful."

As Leonard's son told Barbara, "You are really a mother to us all," and a grandchild, shortly before their wedding, asked Barbara, "Is it too soon to call you grandma?"

Leonard and Barbara actively communicated with their respective families as their relationship developed. This can greatly ease the way for children and grandchildren to accept a new marriage or partners living together. It is unwise to surprise your children with a final decision.

Naomi and David

With David and Naomi, both sets of children have had difficulty accepting the remarriage of their parents. At the beginning, Naomi's daughters found it hard to accept David, as they had been very attached to their father. David's children have had an even harder time accepting the marriage. One daughter used to call David daily, even after he married Naomi, but once she became involved in a committed relationship, her constant need for her father subsided somewhat. But David says that both daughters still speak to him disparagingly of Naomi when they call, referring to her as an "old bitch." When they talk that way, he tells them to "go to hell."

This sad situation may never be happily resolved, but it is good that David stands up for Naomi when his daughters speak negatively of her or their marriage would surely suffer.

Laura and Ed

Ed, age 90, has two sons, five grandchildren, and nine great-grandchildren. His wife, Laura, age 80, has a son and a daughter, a grandson, and two great-grandchildren. From the first, Ed was 100% accepted by Laura's family, and they have been very generous in paying for Laura and Ed's vacation trips. On the other hand, one son of Ed's and his family at first resented Laura, feeling that "no one could take our mother's place."

Despite this resentment, Laura and Ed persisted in arranging pleasant, social contacts with Ed's family. They phoned and wrote often, and arranged gatherings at their home. Gradually, Ed's children came to know Laura and to accept her as their father's new wife but not as a replacement for their mother in their hearts. Laura and Ed's persistence should encourage older couples who at first do not find acceptance from their adult children. They need to understand their children's attachment to a deceased parent and that forming a new bond takes time and effort.

Nancy and Pat

Nancy and Pat are a committed couple who are living separately. Nancy has two daughters, a son, and five grandchildren. Pat has seven children and thirteen grandchildren. Nancy is closer to Pat's children than he is to hers. "Mother is all settled. Mother has her own life," says Nancy, referring to herself while waving her hands expressively. "Pat's children worried about someone taking care of him after their mother's death, and they see me as the caretaker for their daddy."

Often if a parent does not remarry or find a new companion, the children do become the sole caretakers when he or she declines. Adult children who are uneasy about a parent's becoming romantically involved should keep this eventuality in mind.

Nancy often visits her children alone. Pat takes her with him to see his children, and they all take trips together. Nancy showed me a photo of herself with her family. Pat was present when it was taken, but it was a family photo, and no one asked him to join in the picture-taking. "He really isn't part of my family, exactly," explained Nancy. But Nancy was planning to go with Pat to his granddaughter's wedding, and Pat said insistently, "I want you in the picture."

Nancy's children have all accepted her relationship with Pat, except for one resentful daughter. When Nancy sold her family home so she could buy the apartment in the retirement community near Pat's apartment, this daughter and her husband were extremely angry and hurt because Nancy had told them that they would eventually inherit the family home. Now she regrets very much ever saying this. Her advice to others is, "Never promise your home to any of your children. You never know what the future holds."

Donna and Stuart

Stuart and Donna are a married couple with a 26-year age difference between them. He is 90 and she is 64. Donna has no children. Stuart's two sons accept Donna, but his daughter has been resentful toward her father's second marriage and has not been friendly to Donna. The fact that Donna is three years *younger* than Stuart's daughter, and is of a different religious denomination, certainly affects their relationship. Although Donna and this daughter planned a successful party for Stuart's ninetieth birthday, there was still dissension between them.

It can be very difficult for adult children to accept a parent's marrying someone who is close to their own age. I hope parents listen to and recognize their children's uncomfortable feelings, discuss their differences, yet hold firm in their allegiance to their spouses.

Ellen and Ralph

Ellen and Ralph were recently married. Of Ellen's three children, the two who live nearby have met Ralph and get along well with him. But Ralph's four children have not supported or even acknowledged his marriage to Ellen. His oldest daughter once told him, "It was a stupid mistake for you to marry." Ralph has tried to convince his children to change their attitudes, but Ellen says, "I do not feel welcome in his family."

After their mother's death, when these adult children were young, Ralph had married a woman 16 years younger than himself. His new wife disliked the children, and they hated her in return. This unhappy experience might be affecting their attitude toward Ellen.

Gayle and Jim

Gayle and Jim are living together and plan to marry shortly. Gayle, a widow, has a daughter with one child and an unmarried daughter. Although Gayle and her daughters are very close, her unmarried daughter has not established a rapport with Jim, even though he is a very warm and open person who is easy to know and to like. This could be because Jim is ten years younger than Gayle, because she was close to her deceased father, or for the reason that she does not want to share her mother's love and attention.

Jim has a young adult son from whom he is now alienated; they have no contact. Jim attributes this to the influence of his former wife. Also, before he met Gayle, he and his former wife were considering getting back together. His relationship with Gayle must have been a shock and a disappointment to his son. It is almost always the case that children, no matter what age, hope their divorced parents will eventually be reunited. This desire, no matter how unrealistic or impossible it may be, often affects their feelings toward a potential step-parent.

Alienation From a Child

Fifteen couples are described in this book. Of these thirty individuals, three were completely alienated from one or more of their children, having no contact with them at all. I believe this 10% is a reasonable number, but unfortunately a high one.

Seymour has three daughters. The oldest and the youngest are feuding with the middle daughter, while Seymour supports this middle daughter. As a result, he has no contact with two daughters, and it is only the middle one with whom he and **Edna** have a relationship.

Barbara and **Leonard** enjoy close contact with both of Leonard's two children and one of Barbara's daughters. But Barbara is completely alienated from her other daughter, having no contact with her. She gave no explanation for this rift. Perhaps she doesn't understand it herself.

Losing contact with an adult child is not only painful but also socially embarrassing. It doesn't fit the picture of many generations of a happy family, all loving each other and getting along well. There is often the assumption that the alienation must, in some way, be the parent's fault. Most people do not freely share with others this loss of contact with an adult child—we certainly don't read about it in Christmas letters—but probably it is much more common than most of us realize.

Though **Jim**, **Seymour**, and **Barbara** must feel pain from losing their children, they have not let the sadness interfere with their lives. The same can be said for all those individuals whose children have difficulty with their new relationships. Those who have happy, successful partnerships, or those working toward greater compatibility, recognize that their new relationship is vital to them at this time of their lives. It is wonderful when all the children are close and there is full acceptance of the new relationship. Family is so important, and large, happy family gatherings, sometimes involving several generations, can be memorable. But in an imperfect world, mature adults have to learn to accept what is and treasure the love they have for each other.

Some Final Thoughts

Our couples have experienced both positive and negative interactions with their children and grandchildren. Whatever your situation may be, loyalty to your new relationship should be primary. I recently counseled a man who was distraught because his new wife had left him over his obsessive involvement with his adult children's numerous problems.

Good relations with each other's families need to be fostered early. This can be done by honestly communicating with your children as your new relationship develops and by arranging social activities together. Do not surprise your children and grandchildren by suddenly announcing your upcoming marriage to someone they've never heard of. Let them know they are still important in your life and that you do not expect your new partner to replace their parent. Also, inform your children that you have not forgotten them in your will. (See the section about wills and trusts in Chapter 22 for advice about how to provide for your children.) Your children also need to know that, should your health fail, your new partner may be able to help with your care. These communications can help smooth the relations between children and your new partner, making for happier family interactions.

Health and Sexuality

One of the most inspiring things I have learned from the couples interviewed is that physical intimacy is an important and satisfying part of their relationship. And, of course, health, especially in later years, is inextricably tied to sexuality.

A study of the sex life of older Americans, age 60 and older, that was conducted in 1998, revealed that many older people are active sexually. The study found that:

- 71% of men and 51% of women in their 60s were sexually active, while 57% of men and 30% of women in their 70s reported being sexually active. (These percentages might be low because, as well as recently coupled older people, the study included both single individuals and long-married couples.)

- When asked about the emotional satisfaction they receive from their sex life, 74% of sexually active men and 70% of active women said they were as satisfied or even more satisfied than they were in their 40s. (We had quite a few couples who said the same!)

- When older people are not sexually active, it is usually because they lack a partner or because they have a medical condition.

(Study conducted by the *National Council on Aging*, Washington, D.C., as reported on their Web page: ncoa.org/archives/sex-survey.htm.)

The dark side of this sexual activity is that older adults are becoming increasingly vulnerable to infection with HIV (see statistics on page 275.) A blood test for AIDS is a wise precaution before becoming involved sexually.

Physical changes occur gradually as both men and women age. After menopause, women can suffer from vaginal atrophy, which is a thinning of the vaginal wall that can result in pain during or after intercourse. Oral estrogen or estrogen cream applied to the vagina can often alleviate this problem. There is also a decrease in vaginal lubrication, especially if a woman is not taking a form of estrogen. An over-the-counter lubricant applied before intercourse is very helpful.

As men age, they gradually begin to have less firm and less frequent erections and more limited ejaculations. This will vary greatly with the man's health. While impotence is often assumed to be part of the normal aging process, this is not necessarily so. It may reflect the effect of a chronic disease such as diabetes, or other conditions such as arteriosclerosis and hypertension that can affect the blood vessels and therefore the firmness of an erection. Necessary medications can also interfere with sexual function, especially those used to treat heart disease, high blood pressure, depression, and anxiety.

But even with the changes of aging, the impact of diseases, and the effects of drugs, older couples can, to some degree, continue to enjoy a satisfying sex life. Particularly inspiring were three women who had medical problems that one would think could end their chances of being sexually attractive to a partner. **Karin** lost one breast to a mastectomy, **Barbara** lost both breasts to a double mastectomy, and **Naomi** had an ileostomy after suffering from colon cancer. All of these women had these operations before they met their present partners, yet were still attractive to their mates and currently enjoy their sexual lives.

Of course, sex is not just a physical act. It is a supremely bonding force between a loving couple. Our sexuality is a strong component of our relationship and often takes the form of affection, teasing, and laughter. Jerry and I both had seriously ill spouses and long periods of abstinence, so our lovemaking makes up for all the years we lived without it. If continued aging or medical problems catch up with us, we will still be sexual to whatever degree we can, as the bond has been formed.

The couples we interviewed have taught us a great deal about sexuality in later life. For all of them, the return to a sexual life was an important part of their relationship. Here are their stories.

Ruth and Paul

Ruth and Paul, a married couple, first became sexually involved when she was 71 and he was 73. Their first experience together, after many years of abstinence, was not satisfactory. In fact, Ruth described it as "terrible."

With time, trust, and more open communication, Ruth and Paul became more comfortable with each other, and their sex life gradually improved. Now they have sexual activity almost daily, usually after waking in the morning. (For many couples, morning is the prime time for sex, probably because they are rested.) Ruth's initial vaginal dryness is successfully managed with estrogen and she now finds the experience "lovable." They both believe that "sex contributes much to holding a marriage together. It increases the bond between the two of us. We express every day our love for each other."

At age 80 Paul has no problems with erection or ejaculation! This is somewhat unusual, but Paul is active, in good health, and looks to me like a man of 60. He has a slightly enlarged prostate gland that is controlled with medication, but that does not interfere with his enjoyable sex life.

Nancy and Pat

Nancy, age 75, and Pat, 77, are a committed couple living separately. Let Pat tell us how their love life developed:

"The physical attraction to Nancy grew on me naturally. I just got to liking her better and better. I didn't have any idea at first we'd ever do anything sexual. Then one night as we were cuddling up watching television, I just happened to mention, 'I wonder if we could go to bed together.' Laughingly, we ran into the bedroom . . . and so it started."

It was after the beginning of their sex life that Nancy and Pat started to spend nights at each other's homes and to see themselves as a committed couple. With most of those interviewed, their first sexual encounter also marked the beginning of their commitment to each other.

Currently Nancy and Pat have intercourse about twice a week, usually in the morning. At age 77, Pat still is able to hold an erection but doesn't always ejaculate. "I can only charge up my battery twice a week," he said with a smile. Pat feels he is able to enjoy sex more with Nancy than he had with his wife, primarily because during their marriage, as Catholics, they used the rhythm method for contraception. "It didn't work very well—we had seven children. But maybe it did, since we didn't have fourteen!"

Nancy had a hysterectomy at age 45 and takes estrogen. She lubricates naturally and is orgasmic. She suffers from incontinence, however, and has had surgery for this problem. She presently uses pads, but this in no ways turns off Pat sexually. Sex is better for her with Pat than it was with her husband, but at that time, between her husband's work and the raising of three children, their distractions from sexual intimacy were many. For her as a Catholic, the rhythm method was an interference until after her hysterectomy. Also, her husband was more inhibited than Pat. "I'm a very different person now with Pat. We have a very open relationship sexually. He is a great lover. We can talk freely about our love life. I'm very responsive."

Joanne and Andy

Joanne, 59, and Andy, 60, are a younger couple than most of those interviewed. After dating for 14 months, they have now been living together for eight months. They became sexually involved after keeping company for seven weeks. Joanne "held out" that long because Andy had told her that with his participation in singles groups, "The easiest thing in the world was to get laid." She didn't want to be "just another lay." At first, they necked and petted. "It was like being in high school, in the back seat of a car, steaming up the windows," Joanne recalled. "The first time we had intercourse, it wasn't the best sex, but it's been getting better ever since."

Joanne has a stronger sex drive than does Andy. "I take hormones and would like sex almost every day," she said. Andy had a previous bout with cancer, which has lowered his energy level somewhat. They have sex about once a week, and Joanne has learned to accept this. With a pleased look on her face, she exclaimed, "After living five years by myself, I thought I liked sleeping alone. Now I practically sleep on top of him, like a fly on a windshield." Andy, with a glow on his face, added, "Just feeling our bodies close, it's really nice. In the morning when we cuddle and hold each other, to me that's heaven."

Contrary to stereotypes, it is not at all uncommon for women to want intercourse more frequently than men. Closeness in bed, however, which Joanne and Andy so enjoy, is a pleasure that can be savored for many years, despite increasing age and deteriorating health.

Karin and John

Karin and John, like **Pat** and **Nancy**, are a committed couple, living separately. Their intimate relationship began about two years ago. Both are presently in good health, although Karin lost a breast to a mastectomy prior to meeting John. This did not stop

John from finding her desirable, nor did it interfere with their sexual pleasure.

John, who is 69, tends to be a worrier. When discussing sexuality, he expressed concern about his sexual performance. (I dislike that word *performance* when men use it. It detracts from spontaneity and seems to put unnecessary pressure on the man to perform in a particular way.) Karin, who is 65, said she would like sex more frequently. John admitted that he is often tired from such activities as running and dancing, desiring sex less often. He often climaxes before Karin and then satisfies her manually. She expressed the wish that they could climax together during intercourse. When I discussed this with the two of them, they both realized that this goal was based on a myth: it is seldom that both partners climax at the same time.

John was concerned that he no longer could achieve an erection by just thinking about Karin, as he did when he was younger. Men can do this in their teens and early twenties, but certainly not at age 69! His erection now takes longer to attain, but this is no problem if he takes time, relaxes, and caresses Karin. Also, his erection doesn't last as long as it did when he was younger. John needed reassurance that this is all normal as a man ages. As we discussed their sexuality together, John observed that, "If a man doesn't know these facts, he can get scared and then may really not get it up."

Karin on the other hand, has none of John's worries. She described their sexual life as "wonderful, open, and satisfying." Although it had been many years since she had been sexually involved, she has had no problems with urinary tract infections or vaginal dryness. She has multiple orgasms, which John really likes. Although Karin would sometimes like sex when John is not in the mood, she is accepting of his needs and hopes he doesn't feel pressured, which he says he doesn't. When asked about their sexual frequency, they agreed it was usually once or twice a week. They said that the more they are together, the more frequently they are sexual, if they are both rested and not too busy. With a twinkle in his eye, John said, "If my friends read this, tell them we have sex at least three times a week!"

Janice and Cliff

Janice is 55 and Cliff is 67. They are married and have been together as a couple for about eight years. For the first few years, their sexual intercourse was very satisfying, but recently their activity had become "much quieter." Cliff was experiencing a diminished sex drive and was having difficulty maintaining an erection. Cliff expressed the fear that he was impotent and refrained from approaching her because of his performance anxiety. Janice believed that she had lost her attractiveness to him.

Janice said, "Sex has been an important part of our relationship, and I miss it. We both feel insecure about Cliff's condition, knowing that otherwise he is in good health. As his desire decreases, his worry about his performance increases."

During our discussion, Cliff was relieved to learn that problems with erection are common with aging. This knowledge has decreased his anxiety so that now he maintains a firm erection and their sex life is improving. If a man does not understand these natural changes and believes he is impotent, this thought alone is enough to inhibit his erections. Cliff's doctor prescribed Viagra™, which he uses on occasion. Janice is pleased that sex is now more frequent and satisfying. "If I'm not getting enough sex, I'm somewhat edgy." The two also touch, snuggle, kiss, and, at times, mutually masturbate.

Naomi and David

David, age 80, has similar concerns about impotence. He and Naomi, who is 78, a married couple, have been together for 14 years. Naomi told me that when they first became sexually involved, they had an active and enjoyable sex life.

Now approaching 81, David admits sadly that he is impotent. The most likely cause is his blood pressure medication. Recently his dosage was lowered, and Naomi is hopeful that the situation may improve.

His impotence is of great concern to David. He tried a suction pump, but it hurt, and now he wants to try Viagra™, but Naomi is afraid of possible harmful, long-term side effects. Naomi emphasized that David brings her to orgasm by stimulating her manually, and I pointed out that for many women, clitoral stimulation is even more satisfying than intercourse.

Naomi was emphatic about David's concern regarding his lack of erection: "It's no problem for me. It is only a problem for him and it's in his head. We have sex about once a month now, which is good enough for me. I'm not 21 years old. If sex only were what I wanted with David, would our relationship have lasted this long?"

Carol and Ron

Carol, age 64, and Ron, 72, have been together for 17 years. They are married and live separately. When they first became involved, at ages 47 and 65, they had many periods of intense sexual activity. Then, because of a back problem and vaginal pain during intercourse, Carol lost her sex drive and now has no desire for sexual relations. "It hurts too much," she says. "I can't stand it." She attributes her pain and sexual problems to having been molested as a child. She recovered memories of this abuse as an adult, during individual and group therapy.

EDITH

 The theory behind "recovered memories" is that severe physical and sexual abuse is too painful for a child to hold in consciousness. These memories are therefore, dissociated (kept out of consciousness) and recovered in later years, usually during psychotherapy. There is much dispute in the psychotherapeutic community about the validity of this theory. Considering that Carol was left alone and unprotected a great deal as a child, I believe that her memories are likely to be true.

About five years ago, Ron was diagnosed with cancer of the prostate. He had an orchiectomy that removed the testosterone-forming glands from his testicles to retard the spread of the cancer. As a result, he lost his ability to have erections. Thus, Carol and Ron no longer have sexual intercourse, and Ron finds this frustrating. Their feelings for each other are expressed by sitting together, holding hands, and hugging, but no deep kissing, no touching, and no stroking of intimate parts. They sleep together at times, in a companionable way. Carol told me that Ron sees intercourse as the only way of making love, and he is not willing to do other things that she would find exciting and satisfying.

Some Suggestions

Older couples need to know that there are many other ways to achieve sexual arousal and even orgasm other than through intercourse, or in addition to intercourse. The following suggestions may be helpful if they fit with your moral and religious beliefs.

Touching the breast and stimulating the nipple with the hand or tongue can be very exciting. There is a spot right at the bottom of the spine that is erogenous. In fact, tenderly stroking and kissing all parts of the body can be a loving and exciting experience for both the receiver and the giver.

Mutual masturbation with the man gently rubbing the vulva and clitoris with a moist finger, and the woman stroking the penis can often lead to orgasm. The penis, limp or erect, can be rubbed within the exterior vulva and against the clitoris. Then there is oral sex, a very common practice today. In cunnilingus, the man stimulates the woman's outer vagina and clitoris with his tongue. This can be extremely exciting and often the only, or the primary way, that many women achieve orgasm. Fellatio refers to the woman sucking a man's penis. With this procedure, a woman can give her partner excitement and bring him to orgasm. She can withdraw her mouth before ejaculation, if desired. Two references treat this topic:

- *The New Male Sexuality*, by Bernie Zilbergeld, 1992; Bantam Books (particularly pages 108–111 and 357–358)
- *The New Joy of Sex*, edited by Alex Comfort, 1996; Crown Publishers (particularly pages 85–88 and 105–110)

Sexual Behaviors of Our Oldest Couples

Mary and **Fred** married when she was 63 and he was 57. Now she is 85 and he is 79. Previously they had an active sex life, but now they describe it as "nice." They both agree that Fred's erectile capacity is adversely affected because of his medication for heart problems and diabetes. Mary states emphatically that, "Sex is not everything in a marriage." Fred follows with, "We get satisfaction from kissing and holding hands, and also closely embracing each other while in bed."

Laura, age 80, and **Ed**, 90, have been together for twenty years and they related that for both of them, sex at first was "very healthy," with intercourse three to four times a week. Their relationship began when Laura was 60 and Ed was 70. But over time, intercourse has waned with Ed's inability to have an erection. At 90, Ed has had his share of medical problems, particularly with his heart and circulatory system. Now hugs and kisses are more important for expressing their affection.

Stuart is 26 years older than **Donna**. When they were first married, both of them felt their sexual activity was good at two to three times a week. Now, at age 90, Stuart can achieve only a limited erection, and they try for intercourse about once a month. Stuart is in very good health for his age. He has had no surgeries and takes no medication. However, it has become more difficult for Stuart to move into various body positions during intercourse.

Donna however, often feels excited and she misses the sexual activity she shared with Stuart. So she now initiates playfulness through sexual touching. Stuart says, "It's up to her now if she gets the desire and it's great that she is able to initiate some activity."

All three of these oldest couples had frequent intercourse when they married at a fairly late age. Now, for various reasons, their sex life consists primarily of affection and physical closeness. They have had enough years together to enjoy sexual intimacy and become more deeply bonded. The suggestions I offer for sexual practices other than intercourse would not fit for these oldest couples because of their possible conservative orientation, and it might not be necessary because they are content with their love lives as they are.

Some Final Thoughts

All the couples had active and satisfying sexual lives during the early parts of their relationships. For those who married, only those with strong moral and religious convictions against pre-marital sex waited until after marriage to become sexually involved. Some, like **Ruth** and **Paul**, have continued with frequent and enjoyable intercourse until very late in life. Other couples, because of physical problems and medications, no longer have intercourse but still enjoy physical affection and cuddling in bed.

For many of the couples, the frequency of their sexual activity decreased as they aged. A sense of humor can really help when this occurs. One of the men I interviewed told me this story about two men conversing in a barber shop:

"Do you remember the first time you had sex?"

"I can hardly remember the last time I had sex."

"That may be true for you, but I have sex *almost* every day ... *almost* on Monday, *almost* on Tuesday, *almost* on Wednesday. ..."

For older individuals, it is important to remember that certain changes in erectile functioning and ejaculation for the man, and thinning of the vaginal walls and a decrease in lubrication for the woman, are absolutely normal with the aging process. This can greatly relieve anxiety so that the couple may continue to enjoy satisfactory sexual experiences.

CHAPTER 18

Personality Differences and Styles of Conflicts

Over the years I have observed that good partners often have the same level of emotional maturity while being of opposite personality types. Thus, in their togetherness they complement each other.

If one partner is imaginative and spontaneous and the other more down-to-earth and practical, they can give each other balance and add a great deal to each other's lives. One brings new interests and excitement into the partnership; the other offers security and stability. The important thing is to appreciate the differences and all the qualities your partner has to offer, rather than trying to change them into a carbon copy of yourself. Also, different personality types address conflict in different ways, from volatile outbursts to withdrawal. At the end of the chapter, you will find suggested "Dos and Don'ts" for handling conflict.

This chapter addresses the similarities and differences in the personalities of our couples and the ways they approach conflict. Some conflict is inevitable in all relationships, and newly formed older couples, with their longstanding habits and opinions, certainly have plenty of areas for disagreement. Understanding how your partner's personality differs from yours can help you to not become offended when you fail to get the particular reaction you were expecting.

Sometime into my marriage to my late husband, we both took the *Myers-Briggs* personality test to learn more about ourselves. (This test is available online at: www.humanmetrics.com/info-mate/infoMatePass.asp) We discovered that I was highly *intu-*

193

itive. This means that I usually consider the big picture by grasping essential patterns. This certainly fits with my profession as a psychotherapist. My husband scored high on the *sensate* scales, indicating that he used his sight, hearing, and other senses to find out what was actually happening around him. The results showed that he was practical, good at working with facts and examining details, which fit his profession as an engineer. Once when I bought a new outfit, I asked my late husband how he liked it as I stood before him proudly modeling my new dress. I meant the big picture: "How do I look in this dress?" and "What is your overall impression?" but he only saw the small details: "The hem is uneven." and "I like the embroidery on the collar." After learning that he perceived the world as a sensate individual, not seeing the big picture, I felt much less disturbed by his comments about my attire.

Jerry, like my late husband, is much more organized and practical than I am. He brings these abilities into our lives and also into this book. Conversely, I like to think that I've brought more richness and adventure into his life. Often I see or hear of a trip that appeals to me, and my first thought is "Let's go!" Jerry is more hesitant, but if we do go, he enjoys himself immensely.

Though Jerry, like my late husband, is sensate and I am intuitive, we are both very extroverted. In social situations and when speaking in public, each of us has trouble getting a word in edgewise while the other one is talking. This could make for conflict, but knowing each other's behavior in such situations, we find it amusing.

Joanne and Andy

Joanne and Andy are particularly clear about how their differing personality traits are complementary. Joanne describes them as "the show girl and the intellectual." She likes rock music, he prefers classical; he likes artistic foreign films, she prefers American romance and adventure.

Joanne lives and works at a fast pace, which Andy admires but doesn't want to get dragged into because he is slower, more thoughtful, and introspective. She wants to "wind him up"; he wants to "slow her down." But at the same time, they believe they are good for each other. Joanne knows she's a workaholic and appreciates Andy's efforts to get her to relax and ease her sometimes frantic pace.

Joanne prefers to live on a grander scale financially than Andy. He says, "I shop in Target, she shops at Nordstroms." Joanne appreciates Andy's helping her to be more careful in her spending, as she has a tendency to go overboard. Andy appreciates Joanne's helping him to be more expressive. He finds it easier now than ever before to show love and tenderness.

Joanne has a temper and will yell and call Andy names when she is angry; however, she gets over it quickly and doesn't hold grudges. Andy is more self-contained and introspective. He does not show his anger and tends to hold it inside, but Joanne senses his displeasure.

Both Joanne and Andy had problems with their fathers when they were children, yet they respond differently to conflict. This is not unusual. Even children in the same family will develop different personality traits in dealing with their parents. Joanne's father was emotionally volatile and she, in turn, has a short fuse and a quick temper in arguments with Andy. Her marriage to her second husband, who was an explosive man like her father, did not work out at all.

Andy's father was a stern disciplinarian who frequently beat his sons. Andy protected himself as a child by walling himself off from being expressive. Thus, he tends not to show anger, but to hold it inside and express his anger in more subtle ways. He admits, "I can be a bully like my father." Joanne doesn't let him get away with this bullying, and Andy says with admiration, "This woman can't be frightened."

Nancy and Pat

Nancy and Pat took the *Myers-Briggs* test. Nancy is a *sensate* type: practical, organized, and settled. Pat is disorganized, perceptive, and thinks ahead. He is an *intuitive* type who has brought a good deal of excitement into Nancy's life as well as openness and freedom to their sexual experiences. Nancy offers Pat stability and organization, which he gratefully accepts. For example, he gives her his bills to pay and accepts her reminders of appointments without resentment. During their later years, these partners have found in each other the undeveloped parts of themselves.

They claim that they never argue, which is hard to believe, but they assure me that it is true. They do admit to having "heated discussions" at times, such as when Pat sold his house and gave the new owners his washing machine and dishwasher. Then he asked them if he could leave his tent trailer in the garage for three days. When they refused he told Nancy indignantly, "They wouldn't let me do it! After all I've given them."

Nancy was the voice of reason and calmed Pat down. "They paid you $14,000 extra for the house. They must need the space."

Pat replied, "She's more forgiving than I am. And she's nicer than I am. Anyone who pulls something like that on me, I'm through with them. But Nancy got out the phone book and called a towing service." At that point they both laughed, and Pat concluded, "How did I know it was going to be so easy?"

This example points out the difference in their approaches. Pat was indignant and explosive. Without Nancy's calming influence, he might have ended up in an ugly dispute with the buyers of his home. Nancy and Pat were both able to laugh about the situation.

Humor is a great softener of disputes. In addition, the fact that this couple lives separately makes for less of the day-to-day frustrations that cause conflicts.

Ellen and Ralph

Ellen and Ralph had a good deal of conflict in the early "working out" period of their relationship. Their different personality styles became evident during arguments. Ellen said, "During heated discussions, I get verbally aggressive and he gets defensive and quiet. He's analytical and thinks things through much more than I do."

Ralph later confided, "I approach things in a logical way. She's not logical; she's very emotional." To use the *Myers-Briggs* dichotomy, Ellen is a *feeling* type, and Ralph is a *thinking* type. Now that they understand their different types, neither one feels offended by the other's style and their relationship is much improved.

Gayle and Jim

Gayle is extremely energetic, talkative, and constantly on the go. Jim is much quieter and more reserved. Gayle is aware and appreciative of this difference and remarks, "Jim is much more laid back than I am. I jump into things right away. He thinks before he acts. He slows me down to a more reasonable pace, and now I don't get as upset as I used to. I really don't think I would have been open to this sort of change when I was younger. I was too impatient. As you get older, you become more realistic of what can be accomplished in life."

In turn, Jim states, "I used to be less organized than Gayle. I let things go. I was messy. Now I get to important things quicker and am much neater."

Like **Cliff**, Jim credits his partner with helping him to be more aware of his emotional side. "I realize that Gayle has made me more in touch with my tender feelings. She has helped me work through some issues I had buried. Living with her has opened doors for me, giving me more choices and opportunities to grow. I feel at home here with her."

"It's important to relax and to enjoy life," Gayle continued. "Savor the time you have. I've learned from Jim how to take time to play. We sit by the river together and appreciate our lives and our world. Jim has helped me to realize how wonderful life really is."

Gayle and Jim's personality differences have clearly benefited them and enabled them both to relish life. Through their relationship, each has become a more complete and happy person.

Barbara and Leonard

Barbara worked in a setting where she was in charge and managed others. She knew that she could be somewhat bossy, which was often necessary with her probationers. But by living with Leonard (who is more introverted and quieter than Barbara), she has learned to not always give an order. Instead of saying "Do the vacuuming," she asks "Can you please get the vacuuming done?" She finds that a more respectful approach works well and there is little conflict in their marriage.

Edna and Seymour

Seymour is a much more organized person than Edna, who is more intuitive and artistic. She expresses her artistic nature in photography and ceramics. This personality difference has caused some conflict between them. Promptness is very important to Seymour and he gets angry if they are not on time, or even early, for an appointment. Edna believes that being on time can be rude to the host and that they should be a few minutes late. They have learned to compromise and usually arrive close to the scheduled time.

Turning off lights is also important to Seymour. At first, Edna was somewhat casual about making sure that room lights were switched off which struck Seymour as being wasteful. Edna tries to be mindful of the lights but admits that she might slip once in a while. Seymour indicates that now if he sees an unnecessary light on, he turns it off and keeps quiet about it. What a smart man! Some things are not worth the fuss.

Edna tends to be less neat than Seymour. She explained, "When I was bringing up my children, it was more important for me to keep the kids happy than it was to maintain a tidy house." Seymour was used to having an uncluttered home. Now Edna makes an effort to be neater, especially when she is working with ceramics. Seymour helps her by doing the dishes and some of the housework.

Another irritation for Seymour comes from Edna's professional training as a social worker. "When Edna analyzes me, it drives me nutty," Seymour says, "Especially because she is usually right."

Disagreements between Edna and Seymour are usually over small things that are annoying, particularly to Seymour, who becomes moody and introspective. The result is often a period of ignoring each other: not talking, sitting silently while watching television, or even eating meals with no discussion between them. Edna has learned to just ride it out. Eventually the anger subsides and things return to normal again. Sometimes the silence ends with a kiss or flowers from Seymour. Often neither of them is sure why the disagreement arose in the first place. For many couples, it would be almost unbearable to go several days without speaking to each other. But Edna is sensitive to Seymour's need to be left alone when he is upset and this period of silence seems to work out well for them.

Laura and Ed

Laura and Ed are somewhat similar to **Edna** and **Seymour** in the way they handle conflict. Laura blows up over something and then becomes completely silent for an hour or so. When Ed is angry, he clams up for a while and then forgets what it was all about. Like Edna and Seymour, they do not talk things out after the period of silence, but they get over their unhappiness and move on. It is possible that their ages (Laura is 80 and Ed is 90) have something to do with their non-confrontational attitudes. Women of Laura's generation were taught to not question their husbands, and thus a period of silence and then dropping the matter without discussion would not be uncommon.

The decision of whether to raise an issue is an individual one. If you continue to feel resentment and unhappiness, it is important to speak out when you are calm. But at times, you can decide to let the matter slide. It is good to be in touch with your own emotions and your partner's state of mind and to ask yourself, "Is this issue important enough for me to bring up at this time?"

Karin and John

Although Karin and John have disagreements, neither one displays their anger openly, but each can tell when the other is displeased. This often is the case when couples are close. A tone of voice, a facial expression, or body posture can give signs to a sensitive partner that something is wrong. When Karin or John sense a problem, they ask, "What's troubling you?" Then they talk out the disagreement, and neither holds a grudge. Not holding grudges is so important. Learning to forgive and forget is a saving factor in many relationships.

Carol and Ron

Carol and Ron have had many differences and bitter arguments during their 17 years together. They are both strong, opinionated individuals. Living together was difficult because they had different ideas about how to run a home. Carol comments, "He had engineering ideas while I had aesthetic ideas." In their early days together, they had huge arguments about this. Now that they live separately but nearby, things between them run much more smoothly. They respect each other's rules and act as a guest in the other's home.

Carol states, "It's important for me to think over a conflict situation and be cautious about how I approach the subject, depending on the outcome I want. I have learned which buttons of his to push or not to push."

Ron, in turn, comments, "Sometimes she's hard on me. I know her feminist attitude. Therefore, I try to ignore small situations. Over the years, we've learned how to react to each other. We are both opinionated and independent people, but we do care for each other. In spite of differences, we help and support each other."

Indeed, over the years together, Carol and Ron have learned more positive ways of dealing with their differences, and life is much calmer and more pleasant for them now. They have grown together in their beliefs and lifestyle, learning to accept differences and to ignore less important issues.

Dos and Don'ts for Handling Conflict

Our couples have many different ways of handling conflict, and each finds the way that suits them best. In this sense, there are no right or wrong ways to deal with conflict, but there are certain behaviors that are unacceptable.

Physical violence of any kind is completely unacceptable. Women and men need to know that help is available from the police, who now receive improved training in dealing with domestic violence. Professional counseling can also be beneficial.

Battered women's shelters are available as a last resort. I am not aware of any shelters for battered men.

Arguments that take place under the influence of alcohol or drugs are likely to get out of hand. Control of drinking or drug use can be sought through such groups as Alcoholics Anonymous or Narcotics Anonymous.

Some simple rules for handling conflict are:

- *Do not* call each other hurtful names. Name-calling only escalates a disagreement and is a negative distraction from whatever the real issues are.

- *Do not* threaten to leave. This undermines the basic security of the relationship. Be sure you've done all you can to save the partnership. If you are seriously thinking of ending your relationship, be sure you have a workable plan to be on your own. Don't cry wolf. Talk of leaving *only* if you really plan to do so.

- If you are very angry and you think you or your partner could lose control, *do* take a "time out" such as leaving the room or taking a walk until you calm down. Be sure to let your partner know that you will return.

- If you are both calm and think the issue is worth talking about (you might decide some things are not important enough to discuss at all), *do* listen to your partner and try to really hear his or her point of view. Let him or her know that you understand, even if you do not agree. If possible, try to negotiate with each of you giving some ground. Remember, habits are hard to change, especially after many years.

- *Do not* blame. Don't start a sentence with *you*, and don't use *never* or *always*, such as *"You never pay attention to me."* Do use a three-part I statement: (1) Name your feelings, while (2) describing in specific terms the situation that disturbs you. For example, *"I feel hurt when you look away from me as we talk.*" (3) Say concretely the change you desire. *"Please look at me when we converse, as it helps me to feel closer to you."*

- *Do not* hold grudges. *Do* forgive. Affection and humor will heal most wounds.

- *Do* know that your loving relationship is more important than any small issues that bother either of you. Jerry can love me even if I leave the lights on, and I can love him even though his magazines and newspapers cover many table surfaces. He can simply turn off the lights, and I can pick up the papers and magazines. It often is simpler and kinder to take care of what disturbs you rather than trying to change your partner.

Some Final Thoughts

Personality differences can lead to partners complementing each other, with two different halves working together to become a harmonious whole. Some conflict is inescapable and different styles of conflict need to be recognized and accommodated. With love, patience, humor, negotiation, and, primarily, acceptance of your partner for who he or she is, an older couple can form a happy and satisfying new relationship.

CHAPTER 19

Friendships

When two young people get together, they are faced with the task of keeping old friends and developing new friendships as a couple. Does he like her friends? Does she get along with his? Do they make new acquaintances together? Does either one become so involved with the new relationship that he or she neglects old friends?

These questions also apply to older couples. For older partners, friendship is often a more difficult issue. Young people make new acquaintances in both work and school environments. Parents of young children meet other parents. Retired individuals with grown children do not have the same social opportunities, but the need for close ties outside the primary couple's bond exists at all ages.

Friends in Common

Karin and **John** met while ballroom dancing, and before they became a couple, were in the same social circle originating from their dance club. It has been very comfortable for them to continue this association as a twosome.

Gayle and **Jim** were blessed with a lucky coincidence. The first time they met was at Gayle's art gallery. Jim went there early to meet some friends. After having an animated conversation with Gayle, his friends arrived. Surprisingly, they were also close friends of Gayle's. About a month later, Gayle had a dinner party for these same friends and Jim. Their having friends in common made it so much easier for Gayle to make the first move. And so began their close relationship.

Introducing Friends to Your New Partner

Not all couples are fortunate enough to have friends in common before they meet, so it is important to introduce your new love to your acquaintances early in your relationship. It can help reinforce your own positive assessment of your new partner and can be the basis for continued association as your relationship develops.

Shortly after they met, **Ellen** took **Ralph** for a day's drive to visit close friends of hers, who liked Ralph immediately. This approval was important to her, as it was to me when, knowing Jerry less than a month, he joined me at a friend's home for four days, and we all got along famously. Jerry and I are still close with this couple, as are Ellen and Ralph with the friends she introduced him to.

Keeping Friends of the Same Sex

It is important to maintain your closeness with friends of the same sex. This necessitates that each partner, without jealousy, allows the other separate time to maintain these ties

Karin has a number of close women companions with whom she used to go camping. "I don't want to lose my friends," she explained, "because they were important to me before I fell in love and are still important to me. I don't want to be one of those women who gets involved with a man and then drops all her friends. Who knows how long our love will last, but friends are forever." It is good that Karin recognizes this risk of losing old friends and she is wise to maintain them.

Nancy still visits separately with her close women friends, who were part of her women's support group for more than fifteen years. This gives **Pat**, who is somewhat of a loner, his own time, and he appreciates it. Understandably, Nancy doesn't see these friends as often as before she became involved with Pat, but they are still an important part of her life.

The Challenge of Moving to a New Location

When **Mary** and **Fred** first married twenty years ago, she moved into his home, many miles from where she had previously lived. Leaving her son and many good friends behind was a difficult adjustment. They lived in Fred's house for ten years and then they purchased the apartment where they now live. Although this is in the same area as Mary's former home, many of her old companions had either died or moved away, so the process of making new friends has begun all over again. It is interesting that Mary, not Fred, brings up their moves as adjustments. On the whole, women need more social contacts than men, and a move can be more difficult for them.

In an era when adult children move often away and family ties frequently become tenuous, old friends become more and more important to a sense of well-being as we age. There is an increasing trend for groups of friends to move together to a new location, such as a retirement community, thus taking their support systems with them.

The Advantages of Retirement Communities

The reasons for moving to a retirement community are many: wanting to live in a warmer climate; no longer being able to keep up a large family home; escaping the crime, noise, and congestion of a city; no longer being able to drive; needing more social interaction. If several of these factors become real issues, then moving into a community like **Mary** and **Fred's** can be the answer. It was so much easier for Mary and Fred to make new friends because they now live where activities are available and where all the apartments are in one building. Transportation is provided, and they take many trips to stores, restaurants, and theaters, sharing these activities with their new acquaintances. Meals are provided, and they can chose to dine separately or with other residents. **Laura** and **Ed** live in the same type of residence and have also found it relatively easy to make new friends.

Edna and **Seymour** reside in a large retirement community where the houses are spread out over large acreage. Many activities are offered, but they cook their own meals and provide their own transportation for trips outside the community. They play bridge with other couples and invite each other for dinners. They have acquaintances with whom they garden, make ceramics, and play golf. They have lived in the community for four years and, gradually, through these shared activities, have made many close friends.

Shared activities do not always create close friendships. For example, Jerry and I are both active in our rural community, but we have made more casual acquaintances than true friends. Most of the people we meet have lived in our area for many years and have their own well-developed social circles. Although they are very friendly, they do not reach out for new, close ties. In a retirement community, many of the residents are initially in the same boat, newly arrived and searching for friendship. Thus, though a move to a retirement community has the disadvantage of extending distance from old friends, it has the advantage of making it much easier to form new, close associations.

The Benefits of Staying Put

Mary Pipher, in her interesting book *Another Country* (Riverhead Books, 1999), is a passionate advocate of the older adult remaining in his or her own community, near family and old friends, and with an opportunity to know individuals of all generations. She particularly stresses how, in moving away, many older adults lose frequent contact with their children and grandchildren. She writes, "We want the generations to mix together so that the young can give the old joy and the old can give the young wisdom." I heed Phipher's admonition. I have a three-hour drive to my daughter's home and hope not to move farther from her at any future time.

Karin and **John**, and **Joanne** and **Andy**, have remained in their earlier locations. John's cousin lives nearby. He and John run together regularly, and John and Karin socialize with John's cousin and his wife. They also have other old friends in the same community with whom they spend time as couples. They are both particularly close to Karin's best friend and her partner.

Joanne has lived in the same area since childhood and still has many friends that she spends time with. Andy is near his daughter, who visits their home often. She and Joanne have become close.

Although a move to a retirement community may bring many built-in activities, living in a city or a small town offers many diversions as long as one can walk, bike, or drive to them. But a move may become necessary when, among other reasons, one or both partners can no longer drive. In this case, however, children, grandchildren, or friends often are able to visit frequently and to help with transportation.

Though it is certainly possible to make friends in a new location, remaining near old friends may be more advantageous. A recent study emphasizes how lengthy friendships contribute to the positive self-image of older adults.

"Aging adults seek friends who can reduce the discrepancy between their perception of who they are and the negative identity meanings they might receive from family and others."

("Friendship and Social Support: The Importance of Role Identity to Aging Adults," *Social Work*, November 1999, page 529).

As the older adult becomes more dependent, he or she might be treated with less regard by family or recent acquaintances. The old friend who knew him or her during more productive years is more likely to relate in a manner that reinforces the earlier, more positive self-image.

My dearest friend visited me recently. We are both psychotherapists and still have tremendous respect for each other professionally, and often consult on difficult cases. We had a lot of fun reminiscing about the backpacking and river-rafting adventures that we enjoyed together in the past, and which neither of us is physically able to do now. Thus, we reinforced each other's present-day, positive self-identity.

Religious Institutions as Friendship Sources

Donna and **Stuart** live in their own home in a rural community and are very active in their church, which provides their primary social group. Donna smiles when saying, "I feel so accepted by the members of Stuart's church. We've made many good friends since I've joined. They are a great support for Stuart and me."

Edna and **Seymour**, and **Naomi** and **David**, reside in retirement communities and are active in their local synagogues, where they attend services, have made many good friends, and participate in many activities. This subject is covered in more detail in Chapter 20, *Religious Beliefs and Practices*.

When Old Friends Die

One problem with living to a ripe old age is that many good friends die first. Such losses can lead to isolation and depression. Being with a loving partner can help greatly. In our study, three of the men, **Fred**, **Cliff**, and **David** have lost close friends. None of the three has replaced these companions with other new friends. **Fred's** friends had been part of his working life, and he grew apart from them after retirement. **David** was used to doing things with other men and, now that he is unable to fish or play golf, he is no longer in contact with them. He still has one good friend who is living, but neither of them is well enough to visit the other. Instead, they talk on the phone frequently. Although friends have died, **Cliff** still has close ties with his ten brothers. He is lucky to have ten built-in male companions.

Losing close friends through death seems to happen more frequently to men, because men generally die younger than do women. And as men tend to have fewer close ties, the loss can be more severe. I remember when, several years ago, a man I was close to died suddenly of a heart attack. His best friend, who lived 3,000 miles away, was grief-stricken. They had fought together during World War II, and their strong emotional bond had lasted in the intervening fifty years. He believed he would never again have such a close relationship. Certainly the ties men form during wartime are irreplaceable.

I lost one of my dearest friends several years ago. We had been very close when we were both in our twenties. After I moved to California, I saw her only on the rare occasions when I traveled to the East Coast. During the last few years of her life, I knew she had cancer, but during our infrequent phone contacts she always sounded upbeat and hopeful. I was in such denial that I never fully realized she was going to die. Then one day I received a letter from her sister informing me that she had died after several months in a nursing home. I was distraught. What I regretted most was that I had not kept in better touch and had not gone to see her when she was ill.

I learned from this experience. This past year another friend in the Netherlands was in a hospital, soon to die of cancer. I flew to

Holland and had a brief emotional visit with her. The next day she died. I am so glad we had a chance to say goodbye. It was much more important for me to visit while she was still alive than to attend her funeral.

It is vital to keep in touch with close friends from many years past—more than the yearly Christmas letter. That way you can more accurately ascertain the state of your friend's health and be there when needed. Jerry has a good friend who is gradually going downhill with prostate cancer. He visits and phones him frequently. Jerry hopes he will have the opportunity to say goodbye when the time comes.

With cancer there is a chance to say goodbye. This is not so with a sudden heart attack. Still, if you have been in fairly close contact, you should be less regretful about opportunities lost. Grieving is less painful if it is without guilt or remorse. When a good friend dies, take comfort in the memories of your times together and in the joys of your present life.

Men and Friendships

Most of the men I interviewed had far fewer intimate friends than did their mates. All however, appreciated joining their partners' social circles.

Joanne has many friends with whom she spends time. During the nine years that **Andy** was unattached, he joined singles clubs and his only friends were women. He no longer feels comfortable associating with them now that he is in a relationship with Joanne. "I guess I didn't bother much with men friends after my divorce. Now I wish I had," says Andy. Today, Andy enjoys Joanne's wide circle of acquaintances.

Nancy has more intimate friends than **Pat**. He told me he has just his large family and Nancy. "Nancy's the only friend I need," he explained, but he is becoming closer with a few couples who were originally Nancy's friends.

Carol has many friends from where she previously lived, and they visit each other for as much as a week at a time. **Ron** has few friends but enjoys getting together with Carol's. He prefers working around the house and in the garden during the day and then reading and watching television in the evening.

Like Ron, Jerry is content to work in our orchard during the day and then spend a quiet evening at home. In many ways, this is an advantage and I marvel at how self-sufficient he is. Many of the men I interviewed are equally content to be at home, either alone or with their partners.

My late husband had only one close male friend, a sailing companion. Early in our marriage, he often spoke to me of missing the friendship of men. Eventually, he joined a small weekly men's group. When he first heard of such a gathering, he wondered what activities they participated in. Did they bowl or go fishing? He couldn't imagine that men could just sit around and talk, sharing experiences, problems, and accomplishments. For many years, however, until his death, this small group of men was a central part of his life. Such a group is leaderless and not difficult to form. I strongly recommend to men that if they miss the close friendship of other men, they consider forming such a group. With my first husband, the friendship of these men greatly enriched his life, thereby benefiting our relationship.

Some Final Thoughts

As seniors age, they often want to be not only with family, but also with old friends who share their interests and memories of past experiences. As we grow older, we lose friends through illness and death. Moving to a new community can mean the loss of old friends and gradually the acquisition of new acquaintances. Retirement communities bring together many older people who may be eager to form new ties. For some, staying in the area where they have lived for many years means keeping active their long-term connections with family and friends. When one member of a couple is well-established, the new partner often moves into a ready-made social circle.

For both partners, when the union is a good one, the joy of being with each other can outweigh any difficulties incurred in forming new friendships. But no two people, no matter how much they are in love, are an island unto themselves. Pleasure can be found by spending time with other couples. Individual friendships help to keep the necessary balance of separateness and togetherness in a relationship. Without doubt, establishing and maintaining genuine friendships remain vital to an older couple in a new relationship.

CHAPTER 20

Religious Beliefs and Practices

Membership in a religious congregation can provide a vital sense of community as well as a social life, while members support each other through difficult times. Belief in God and an afterlife can offer comfort in the face of hardship and death. Research shows that faith helps individuals live longer. One study followed more than 5,000 Californians for twenty-eight years. Those who attended religious services at least once a week had a 23% lower risk of dying during the study period than those who attended less frequently, even after the researchers controlled for lifestyle factors and social support (*Journal of Public Health*, June 1997, page 48).

Many of those interviewed for this book belong to a church or a temple and, for some, religion is a central aspect of their lives. On the other hand, those who have no religious associations also do well in their lives, with other ethical convictions and activities sustaining them. Among our couples, affiliations include fundamentalist Christian, mainstream Protestant, Catholic, and Jewish faiths. While most believe in God and an afterlife, some are agnostic. Beliefs also include reincarnation, the Goddess religion, and the importance of humanitarian values. While many of the individuals interviewed came from the same or similar denominations as their partner, others held different belief systems but were respectful of each other's religious views. Let us examine this very important aspect of newly coupled, older couples' lives.

Stuart and Donna

Before their marriage, Stuart and Donna were members of different conservative Christian groups. In the beginning stages of their relationship, Stuart expressed concern that Donna was of a different denomination, but their religious beliefs were not that far apart. During their courtship together, they attended services at each other's churches.

Once married, Donna converted to Stuart's church, where they are both very involved with the congregation. Their church is active worldwide and takes care of its members in many ways. In his will, Stuart is leaving his house not to Donna or to his children, but to his church. In return, he sees no need for long-term-care insurance as he knows his church will take care of him and Donna, should it be needed.

Ruth and Paul

As a child, Paul was teased because his family belonged to a minority Christian group. But it remained important to him, and he continues to worship in a local church of that same denomination. He is active in its congregation, and it is an important part of his life.

Ruth had shifted from one Christian belief to another during her youth and through her first marriage. Now she attends services at her husband's church, but has not joined the congregation. She believes in the Golden Rule and in the teachings of Jesus Christ, recognizing "the wonders of this wonderful world that God has given us."

Edna and Seymour

Seymour is Jewish and feels strongly about practicing his faith. He has a firm allegiance to Israel, where one of his sisters lives and where his parents are buried. For years, he was active in a Conservative congregation, but the temple he and Edna attend in their retirement community is Reformed and has no permanent rabbi.

Although she attends services with Seymour, Edna is not a member of any church or temple. She believes in living by the Golden Rule: "Do unto others as you would have them do unto you." Edna also believes in past lives and what can be learned about people from studying their astrological signs. She seldom discusses these beliefs with Seymour and, although he doesn't share her beliefs, he does respect her right to have them. Edna would convert, but Seymour doesn't believe it is important for her to do so. She participates in religious services and finds the moral, caring beliefs of Judaism readily acceptable to her. In accordance with these convictions, they both work in a shelter for the homeless that is under the auspices of a Jewish organization.

Edna and Seymour's recognition of each other's spiritual traditions is exemplified by their celebration of Christmas, Hanukkah, Passover, and Easter. All the generations gather to celebrate these holidays together, demonstrating a wholesome acceptance of each other's religious heritages. At Hanukkah and Christmas time, gifts are exchanged, however they have no Christmas tree. Although the tree was important in Edna's childhood, it is unacceptable to Seymour. They do, however, display a menorah and light the candles during the eight days of the festival of Hanukkah.

Mary and Fred

Mary and Fred are another couple from different denominational backgrounds but who respect each other's beliefs. Fred was raised Catholic and Mary Protestant. They each attend their own church and sometimes go to each other's services. Both believe that religion is essential "to keep people fair and honest."

Nancy and Pat

Both Pat and Nancy are Catholic and became acquainted through their church. Pat doesn't consider himself as strong a Catholic as Nancy is, but he goes to church every Sunday to be with her. He says happily, "Nancy's going to get me into Heaven one way or the other. She prays for me. I can't miss. All I have to do is be nice to Nancy from now on and not kick the dog." (Neither one has a dog!)

Nancy and Pat are not married. I asked Nancy how her relationship with Pat has been accepted by their congregation and how it fits with her religious convictions. Nancy tells me that they walk into church every Sunday holding hands. No one has ever said anything, and she hasn't offered any explanation. She told me, "Our partnership is so right. The whole purpose of love is the ultimate sharing. We haven't hurt anyone. We don't have to worry about birth control. I have not talked with anyone about our relationship from a spiritual point of view, because I know it's right for me. It's our conscience that is our ultimate guide. We take care of each other, and we make each other so happy. We're committed."

Naomi and David

Naomi and David are another example of a couple for whom religion is central to their lives. They are both very active in their Reformed Jewish temple and, in fact, David and Naomi met at a temple service.

David was raised in an orthodox Jewish orphanage, where he learned Hebrew. Naomi read stories and histories of the Jewish people and learned to read and write Hebrew. However, she was not taught to believe in God. Today, she believes that there might be a God.

Carol and Ron

Carol had few religious experiences as a youth or during her marriages. Ron was brought up as an Episcopalian, but he did not continue to observe his faith in later life.

Now they both have a strong interest in a nondenominational religious philosophy and together attend a church espousing this philosophy, while honoring all deities. As Ron explained, "What we have now follows beliefs I have held most of my life. Each person is in control of what happens to him or her. If the person thinks positively about something, it will happen. You are what you believe, and you can be whatever you want. The responsibility for beliefs and actions rests with each individual."

Carol also has become very involved with these concepts. She attends a Positive Living Center with Ron. Previously, she considered herself an atheist. Now she reads about religions extensively and strongly believes in self-healing and psychic phenomena.

Gayle and Jim

As a child, Gayle was baptized Episcopalian, while Jim considers himself a "recovering Catholic." Today they both attend, as do **Carol** and **Ron**, a Positive Living Center that teaches "If you relate to the world with a positive attitude, it affects how you function and what life means to you."

Joanne and Andy

Like **Nancy** and **Pat**, Joanne and Andy were raised Catholic; however, it was their mutual identification as "strayed Catholics" that attracted them to each other. Their similar religious upbringings and their parting from the church were part of what bonded them. Both are still influenced by their upbringing, keeping faith with their belief in a Divine Being and an afterlife.

Janice and Cliff

Janice was raised Catholic, while Cliff's family attended the Lutheran church. At present, neither one is involved with any particular religion, but they are searching. Janice wants a spiritual connection because both she and Cliff are "fairly spiritual. We believe in God." She also believes in reincarnation and karma: what goes around, comes around. In her own words, "We all have responsibilities to the planet and to other people living here." Janice believes strongly that she and Cliff had "been together in a previous life." They both believe in having lives previous to the present ones.

Cliff shares Janice's spiritual views by being open about religions, believing in forgiveness, tolerance, and accepting alternative lifestyles. He prefers sermons with intellectual substance and has attended various services during holiday periods to learn about their message and what needs they serve in the community.

Other Non-Attending Couples

Like **Joanne** and **Andy**, and **Janice** and **Cliff**, several other couples interviewed do not attend any church or temple. **Barbara** and **Leonard** describe themselves as agnostic, although Barbara strongly believes that her friends' prayers helped her recover from cancer.

Laura and **Ed** watch services on television. Ed has had many severe medical problems, so this way of participating in religion is understandable.

Some Final Thoughts

All the individuals interviewed have found their own unique paths to the kinds of worship, or non-worship, that suit them. Some couples are solidly together in their beliefs, attending the same church.

Others have different religious affiliations but respect this dissimilarity in the same way that they recognize and honor other differences between themselves. This togetherness in faith, or a tolerance of dissimilar beliefs, contributes to a successful partnership when older couples are forming or involved in new relationships.

CHAPTER 21

Monetary and Legal Arrangements, Including Thoughts About the End of Life

This chapter discusses the financial and legal arrangements made by the couples interviewed. It is divided into two parts. The first is about how to share ongoing expenses, including house payments, utilities, food, entertainment, and travel. The second part deals with specifying how and to whom assets are left after death and the legal instruments such as wills, trusts, and premarital agreements that come into play. (See Chapter 22 for descriptions of these instruments.)

As I discussed legal matters with our couples, we also considered whether the woman had changed her name and whether the couple may have made decisions about purchasing long-term-care insurance. Finally, attitudes concerning the end of life were explored, including whether to allow life to end in the event of a terminal illness. All these concerns are examined in this chapter.

Ongoing Expenses

The decision about how to share expenses often is made early in the relationship, beginning with expenses surrounding dining out and then extending to all living expenses as the couple becomes more deeply involved. For couples who live separately, this matter is less complicated, as household expenses are not involved.

Nancy and **Pat**, who are unmarried but very much committed to each other, live separately in two identical, small apartments in a retirement community. Each pays their own home expenses, and the host or hostess provides the meals when they visit each other's apartments. When they go out, they take turns treating each other, and when traveling, they split all expenses evenly.

Karin and **John** are also not married and live separately. Karin is better off financially than John, and she is perfectly content to cover more costs when they do things together. Karin must battle with John in order to pay her share of dinners, movies, and other entertainment, because he wants to pay it all as a matter of masculine pride. Being the partner with less money is sometimes difficult for John. John wants to live with Karin and pay something toward her townhouse expenses, but she is hesitant. Vacations present a problem, as Karin can afford more expensive trips than can John. As a solution, they plan to travel as reasonably as possible, and Karin accepts it that way.

Joanne and **Andy** are unmarried, living together, and Joanne is still actively consulting in her field, while Andy is retired. Despite Joanne's income being greater than Andy's, they share expenses equally. They have separate checking accounts, they split the rent and utilities equally, and put money in a basket to use for food and household expenses. Like **Karin** and **John**, the only time they have difficulties with this difference in income is when they go out or travel.

David and **Naomi**, **Laura** and **Ed**, and **Ellen** and **Ralph** are three married couples who share their living expenses equally. Because Naomi has considerably more financial resources than David, she bought their present home in a retirement community and she pays the maintenance costs. To equalize matters, David pays for their food and utilities, and they split travel and entertainment expenses.

Ellen and **Ralph** use the same method. When they lived in Ralph's apartment, he paid the home expenses, and Ellen took care of all groceries, the phone, and other living expenses. They now live and travel in a recreational vehicle that they bought together with their accumulated savings and the proceeds from the sale of Ralph's home.

Laura and **Ed** have a slight variation in handling expenses. They put the same amount monthly into a joint checking account for all their expenses, but Laura reimburses this account for personal expenses such as clothing.

Mary and **Fred** are a married couple, with Fred having the majority income. Mary receives Social Security benefits that are kept in a separate bank account and which she uses for her personal needs. This gives her a certain degree of independence, although Fred pays for their major living expenses. When the man holds the purse strings, it is sometimes he who has more power in the relationship. This appears to be the case with Mary and Fred and also with **Donna** and **Stuart**.

In the case of **Ruth** and **Paul**, Paul is wealthier than Ruth, yet they equally divide expenses and share decision-making. Ruth owns the home in which they live, and they split their utility and home-maintenance charges. Paul pays the larger bills for major purchases, travel, and dining out, while Ruth handles the costs for groceries.

Gayle and **Jim** are a younger couple who are living together, though not married. Gayle is better off financially than Jim. Gayle owns their house and pays for food and travel expenses. Jim handles only the utilities and the telephone bills, while he pays off previous debts. As long as Jim works freelance, Gayle encourages him to put any excess income he has into investments to benefit himself. Gayle manages their financial accounts. This is an artistic couple with new-age beliefs, and they are both comfortable with the woman being the older and wealthier partner.

Conflicts Over Spending

It is important to look at different attitudes about spending. For **Laura** and **Ed**, money is a major issue. Laura likes to buy things on the spur of the moment, which Ed often thinks are frivolous. However, Laura has money of her own, and they share their living expenses equally. There is still some conflict between them when she buys something expensive *even with her own money.*

Part of Ed's attitude could be left over from growing up during the Depression of the 1930s, and part of it could be because he and his first wife planned their purchases together. Laura always made independent decisions about purchases, even during her prior marriage. Thus, Laura and Ed's previous spending patterns differ, and their behaviors and attitudes are carried over into their present relationship.

Couples need to look at previous patterns to better understand and accept present differences and update their attitudes. Laura now buys what she wants, and Fred is learning to accept her right to her independence.

Ruth and **Paul** are another example of different attitudes about money. In this case, Ruth is more frugal than her husband. Paul is more affluent than Ruth and is accustomed to spending money more freely. As a result of Paul's past business experience, he uses the telephone a great deal and makes lengthy calls. This bothers Ruth. At first they took turns paying the telephone bill, but now if a bill is excessive, Paul pays the extra amount. Paul often allows lights to continue burning after he leaves a room. Ruth reminds him of this, but he often forgets. She now turns the lights off without comment, and he pays excessively high utility charges. By taking responsibility for added telephone and light costs, Paul has diffused any potential conflict with Ruth, and she is still free to hold her belief regarding the spending of money. She says, "By living through the Depression years of the 1930s, my generation learned the value of a dollar, and we are still careful with our purchases."

Inheritance

Our couples vary as to whom they will leave their assets. Some plan to leave money and property to each other. Others, knowing their partners are financially self-sufficient, provide inheritances for their children, grandchildren, or other relatives.

Assets Left to Children

Nancy and **Pat** each have a living trust that leaves assets to their children. **Karin** and **John** also have arranged inheritances for their children. Karin has a will, leaving all of her assets to her children and grandchildren. John has no trust or will, as there would be little to divide among his children. He believes that they will manage matters involving the sharing of his limited estate without conflict.

Laura and **Ed** have a premarital agreement and separate trusts, providing that assets acquired before their marriage stay with each individual and are inherited by each one's children and grandchildren.

Though **Bill** has established a living trust, leaving his assets to his children, he is putting aside a percentage of his investments for **Joyce** in case he dies first. It is encouraging that despite their difficult relationship, Bill wants to help Joyce with her future financial security.

Assets Left to Each Other

Some couples leave their assets primarily to each other rather than to their children. **Mary** and **Fred** have named each other as primary inheritors, using a prenuptial agreement, separate wills, and living trusts. After both of their deaths, their assets will pass proportionately to each one's daughter and on to their grandchildren.

Carol and **Ron** have also established living trusts, leaving their assets to each other. Carol has no children, and Ron has one daughter. Ron feels certain that his greater income would comfortably take care of Carol should he die first, because her own funds are decreasing. Ron's daughter would be the heir in his will after Carol, and he has left her a small portion of his estate upon his death.

Ellen and **Ralph** also name each other as beneficiaries. Each one has established a living trust and a will for this purpose. Ellen does not think that her children will need her money, while Ralph believes it is more important to leave assets to Ellen than to his children. This is an example of how each considers their own relationship primary and that with their children secondary. It fits with the lack of acceptance of the marriage by Ralph's children and Ellen's limited contact with her three children.

Three of the women have given their partners the right to remain in their homes even though the properties eventually will pass to their children. Each has arranged this differently.

Naomi, through her living trust, allows **David** to remain in the house and provides that the first $600,000 of her estate will be divided among her children and grandchildren; the rest will be left to David until he dies.

Janice and **Cliff** have established a postnuptial agreement that passes on their assets as stated in each of their wills. Janice has an interesting way of dividing her funds after her death: her brother, as trustee, will distribute her estate according to the needs of the inheritors, but her will allows Cliff to remain in the house until his death.

Barbara has used a prenuptial agreement to ensure that upon her death, **Leonard** may continue to live in the house as long as he wishes before her daughter acquires it.

The Woman's Name Change

This matter can be a part of legal arrangements after marriage. Whether a woman changes her name to her husband's depends greatly upon the woman's outlook on life and her sense of identity.

Donna, a very traditional Christian lady, not only changed her name without question, but very much resents being addressed by mail as Ms rather than Mrs.

Laura, Mary, Ruth, and **Naomi** all have taken their husband's names. **Barbara** has kept all of her property in her former name, but has changed the surname on her driver's license and Social Security account. **Ellen** has been phasing out her previous surname for personal use, business matters, and on legal documents, replacing it with her new, married name. Ellen's extra effort in changing her name shows her basic traditional outlook, despite the fact that she is very independent as a businesswoman.

Two of the women decided not to change their names. **Carol** has kept her maiden name and does not use **Ron's** surname at all. This is acceptable to Ron. **Janice** has kept her maiden surname, which she re-established after her divorce. It is the name she has used in her professional life and she still uses it for identification on her driver's license, bank account, and Social Security account. For some purposes, she uses this name hyphenated with **Cliff's** surname, but mostly it is important to her sense of identity to keep her maiden name.

Like Janice, my own name use is a compromise. I have kept my previous married name, *Ankersmit*, on all identifying documents and investments. Keeping this name is particularly important to me professionally. I often use *Ankersmit Kemp*, as shown on the title page of this book. Socially, I respond to *Edith Kemp*.

Power of Attorney for Health Care

This is an important document that each individual should complete. It specifies your wishes regarding being kept alive in the event of a terminal illness and who has the right to make this decision. For unmarried couples, this form is essential, as without this document, neither individual would have any say regarding his or her partner's medical treatment. See page 239 for additional information.

Nancy does not want to be kept alive unnaturally and has completed this form, although her partner, **Pat**, has not done so. **Barbara** and **Leonard** have each signed Power of Attorney for Healthcare forms so that each can make life-support decisions for the other. In the document, Barbara's daughter and Leonard's son follow each of them with the decision-making power.

Janice and **Cliff** also have completed this form. Janice is the executor for Cliff, and her brother is her executor. Neither wants "any medical heroics" in the event one or the other becomes terminally ill. They will donate any usable organs to an appropriate organization.

While **Laura** and **Ed** have not prepared the Power of Attorney for Health Care forms, they both have understandings with their children about limiting their terminal care. After our discussion, they agreed to consider completing such a document, as it would ensure better legal compliance with their wishes.

Long-Term-Care Insurance

The pros and cons of acquiring long-term-care insurance are discussed in Chapter 22. Our couples vary in assessing the need for this insurance. Age, health, and financial circumstances all contribute to their decisions.

Pat has long-term-care insurance, but his partner, **Nancy**, does not. Pat does not want to burden his children with his care and he is aware that, with his failing eyesight, if Nancy dies first, he may need assistance. Nancy is in good health and believes that it is unlikely that she will require extended nursing-home care.

Naomi has provided this insurance for **David**, who is already suffering with serious health problems and memory loss. But he says, "I'm not going to need it." He does not want to think of this eventuality. Few of us do. Naomi does not believe that she needs such insurance, as she has sufficient assets to cover her care.

Barbara and Leonard both have long-term-care insurance, having purchased it separately when they were younger and it was less expensive. They do not want their children to be forced to care for them.

Both **Gayle** and **Jim** have long-term-care insurance. A financial planner recommended it to Gayle and she acquired it through her deceased husband's company plan. Jim purchased this insurance because, at his younger age, it was relatively inexpensive.

Laura and **Ed**, ages 80 and 90, believe this insurance is too expensive for consideration at their advanced ages. The reader needs to determine his or her own perceived need for this insurance against whatever the cost might be.

Attitudes Toward the End of Life

All of our couples know that their time together is limited and precious. The title of **Joanne** and **Andy's** interview chapter, *"Life is Short, Eat Dessert First,"* exemplifies this belief. But the attitudes of our couples toward eventual death differ.

Nancy and **Pat** are very aware of their increasing ages and have discussed both illness and death extensively. They wonder who will go first. Pat laughed and said, "I hope it will be in the middle of sex," and then he continued seriously, "One of us is going to be alone. Living in this retirement community will be very helpful at that time." He thinks Nancy will be the better survivor, as she is more practical and better organized.

Carol and **Ron** have also discussed this topic. Ron says, "I'm ready. But I believe I'll come back at a later time." Carol thinks she will die before Ron because, "Ron is a long-termer."

Carol says that she believes in an afterlife and is not fearful of death. She states, "The soul leaves the body and is transported to another world." This gives her a strong desire to make sure that Ron's body is handled properly when he dies; in her words, "so he is not mistreated when he passes on to another world."

When asked about whether she thinks at all about death, **Laura** says, "It does enter my mind," while **Ed** says, "It doesn't frighten me." They agree that "time is running out, and we never know who will go first."

Gayle says that she thinks about death often because of the sudden death of her husband and the injuries **Jim** received in a car accident while she was driving. She expects to live to be 100 because many of her relatives lived into their late nineties. Gayle and Jim each express concern about one dying first and leaving the other to grieve alone. Gayle, with her spiritual beliefs, states humorously, "When I die, I will return as an angel, sit on people's shoulders, and tell them what to do."

When asked about facing the end of life, **Mary** prays that she will go first, while **Fred** said, "If life becomes more pain than pleasure, I want to go and have no one stop me. I'll probably request sleeping tablets from my doctor." This brings up the controversy of assisted suicide, at present illegal in all states but Oregon. Unless laws change, Fred would not be able to get a large quantity of sleeping pills from his doctor.

Paul and **Ruth** have a somewhat different attitude toward death. Paul, smiling, said, "Maybe we'll both live to one hundred. It would be a shame to quit sooner when we are so close." Ruth, smiling, nodded her head in agreement.

Cliff has an outlook similar to Paul's. He does not think much about death. In his words, "Life is too full to really be concerned with death. But when it does come, I won't be fearful of it." **Janice** often thinks about the end of life because her parents are aging, and some close friends have recently died. This discussion caused her to again express her regrets about not having had children. Janice and Cliff both would like to die together. Cliff expresses the concern, "What would happen to me if Janice goes first?"

Barbara and **Leonard** said that they talk about death and an afterlife at times, but Barbara stated, "I don't want to even think about death. We're not concerned with who goes first. We'll face things as they come. I don't want to cross that bridge until it's necessary." Leonard agreed.

Paul, Ruth, Cliff, Leonard, and **Barbara** exemplify the attitude that life in the present is too full and happy to spend much time thinking about death. Despite their older age and the knowledge that life ends sooner or later, they feel young, and death still seems far away. Since I've been with Jerry, despite my years, I feel inside like a young girl in love. I know someday we each will die, but I hope it will be many years from now.

By their preparation of wills and trusts, our couples have acknowledged in a practical way the inevitability of death. For some, thoughts of life ending are very much in mind. Others do not wish to contemplate death, focusing rather on present joys. For most, beliefs and attitudes about eventual death are an essential part of their perspectives on life.

Some Final Thoughts

Money management is a crucial ingredient in any union, and partners need to work out what suits them best. A Citi Bank survey finds that "57% of all divorces stem from arguments over money" (*Time* magazine, June 25, 1999, page 80). This statistic emphasizes how important it is to be clear with your partner about how expenses are to be shared and to whom resources are willed.

Each of our couples has their own unique way of sharing expenses and providing inheritances. They also vary in their thoughts about the end of life and in making decisions concerning name change, Power of Attorney for Health Care, and long-term-care insurance.

We recommend that you consider our couples' experiences and discuss alternatives with your partner. By sharing these important and personal matters, your relationship will become closer and stronger.

The following chapter provides important factual information to help you with your decisions regarding legal, financial, and other matters.

CHAPTER 22

Financial and Legal Documents, and Living Arrangements

The following is a brief orientation to documents and procedures that may be useful as an older couple considers their financial and legal situation. A list of references is included at the end of the chapter. You can acquire further information and make important decisions in consultation with financial and legal advisors. But first, try your hand at answering these questions.

1. What are the financial advantages and disadvantages of marrying?

2. Why should you have a will?

3. What is the difference between a will and a living trust?

4. What is a durable power of attorney, and how does it differ from a power of attorney for health care?

5. What are the reasons for acquiring title to property as tenants in common or as joint tenants?

6. Do you recognize the benefits of having a nuptial agreement?

7. What are the alternatives available for retirement living facilities?

8. Should you consider acquiring long-term-care insurance?

Were you able to answer each question with confidence and correct information? Understanding these topics will be important to you now or in the future. As you proceed through the chapter, see how your answers match the information presented.

Financial Considerations and Marriage

There are a number of financial advantages for couples to live together without marriage. A major reason is that when each person has a sizable income, the couple, filing jointly, may find themselves in a higher tax bracket. This is known as the *marriage penalty*. (Since the time of this writing, Congress may have changed this regulation.) A new marriage also can mean the forfeiture of a deceased spouse's pension rights and medical coverage.

Two single persons living together may find that their separate Social Security benefits are subject to less taxation than they would have if they were married. If a spouse dies and you remarry before age 60, you may lose any benefits due, whereas usually there is no loss if you wait until after your sixtieth birthday to remarry. (This is why **Gayle** is holding off her marriage to **Jim** until she turns 60.)

Another reason for remaining single is that a married couple has to spend a significant portion of their jointly owned assets before Medicaid will pay the cost of long-term, nursing-home care for a sick spouse. The assets of the healthy partner of an unmarried couple are not counted in the eligibility criteria for the ill person.

Often, partners do not marry for the above reasons. The Census Bureau indicates that the percentage of cohabiting, unmarried couples has doubled since 1980, and older couples are comprising a large share of this number. It is estimated that, in the United States, 370,000 men and women over 65 lived together without marriage (*Money* magazine, July 1995), and that number continues to grow.

On the other hand, we should not neglect some of the material advantages for being married:

- If you have lived in your home for at least two years, you can sell it and keep up to $250,000 in profit, tax free. For a married couple, the exclusion is $500,000.

- Social Security, company benefits and pension plans, inheritances, and other monetary advantages exist for married couples. (Be sure to add your spouse to your retirement plan as soon as you marry, or you may face a financial penalty.)

- If one married member has significantly more income to draw from than the other, the spousal deduction grants income tax benefits.

- Estate inheritance taxes are avoided because of the unlimited marital deduction on the death of a spouse.

- If one person has health insurance as part of retirement benefits, the spouse can be added. (This also should be done very soon after marriage, or there could be a delay penalty.)

While considering financial advantages and disadvantages of being married, such material concerns should be weighed against moral and/or religious convictions.

Nuptial Agreements

An agreement between two persons prior to their marriage is most often called a premarital or prenuptial agreement. It specifies what will happen to assets in the event of a death. The agreement is used to accomplish one or more purposes:

- Specify property and assets that each person brings to the marriage that will continue to remain his or her separate property.

- Avoid the effect of the community-property law in states having such laws. The chief advantage here is if a partner is still working, earnings remain under his or her control rather than becoming community property.

A premarital agreement must be in writing and signed by both parties. It should be recorded in the county in which the property affected by the agreement is located.

During a marriage, it is common for assets to become community property, jointly owned by both spouses. But a postnuptial agreement also can be made between a husband and wife. It serves the same purposes as does a prenuptial agreement in keeping assets separate.

Wills

A will is a legal document that must be followed in disposing of a person's properties and debts following death. If you die without a will, the laws of your state decide how these matters will be handled. Everything you own could go to your new spouse. Then, when your spouse dies, everything would go to his or her family, not to your children. Because state community-property laws guide inheritance only for married couples, it is particularly important for unmarried couples to have wills or a trust. An executor, named in the will, handles distribution of the estate's assets to the heirs.

In order for a will to be valid, it must be executed in compliance with the law, including signatures of witnesses. Review your will periodically and especially whenever a new, significant life event occurs. If you wish to revoke or change a will, it can be superseded by a new will, or you can make changes through a handwritten and witnessed *codicil*.

A will that is established if you already have a revocable living trust (see Trusts section) is called a *Pourover Will*. If you do not have a trust, it is simply called a will. A pourover will states that your assets are to be distributed by the trust. The advantages of a pourover will is that if you neglected to put something in the trust, it can be distributed as the will provides. Items that have no title, such as jewelry, furniture, artwork, or clothing, can be listed in your pourover will. (Stocks, bonds, real property, and even an automobile with a pink ownership slip have titles and can be included in a trust.)

Power of Attorney for Health Care (Sometimes Called a Living Will)

This document provides instructions for medical care if you become terminally ill and are unable to express your wishes. It answers such questions as: Do you want pain medication or invasive procedures? Do you want to be kept alive through life support? A living will allows you to appoint someone to be your decision-maker if you cannot speak for yourself. This document can help relieve emotional stress for relatives who may be required to make painful decisions. It is particularly important for committed couples who are not married. I knew when I was living with Jerry before we married that, should he become ill, I would have had absolutely no say as to his care without such a document.

Be sure that the original, signed form is either given to the person named to act for you, or that the individual knows where it is kept. Also, provide a copy for your doctor.

Durable Power of Attorney for Financial Matters

This document authorizes someone you specify to act for you if you should become mentally incapacitated and unable to take actions yourself. It gives the authorized person (called an attorney-in-fact) the right to handle your estate and make financial decisions on your behalf. The term *durable* is included because the authorization remains valid even if the signer (you) becomes legally incompetent to act. Your attorney-in-fact has the right to handle financial matters for you in an emergency, including if you are out of the country. Only assets not in your trust can be handled through this authorization for durable power of attorney.

Trusts

Living Trust

A trust is similar to a will, with certain important differences. While a will takes effect when a person dies, a living trust can be set up and used to manage assets during one's lifetime. It is common for the trustor (the person setting up the trust) and the trustee (the person managing the trust) to be the same person. Almost any assets can be placed in a trust—bank accounts, investments, real estate, life insurance, and personal property. When establishing a trust, you change the name or title of each asset to the name of the trust, often with you and your spouse as initial trustees, along with a specified successor trustee. (Example: *Kemp Living Trust, Jerrold E. Kemp, Trustee, Edith Ankersmit Kemp, Trustee, and Andrew Baker, Successor Trustee.*) Then you, as trustee, can manage the assets in your trust during your lifetime.

With a trust, the person gives the designated successor trustee power to continue handling the assets even long after death. A will is a public record for anyone to see and requires that the estate pass through the court probate process before the assets can be assigned to the designated heirs. A trust provides *total privacy* and *avoids probate*—the trust's most important, beneficial features. Going through the legal process of probate is costly and can take many months.

A trust is of value for persons on all economic levels. Various types of trusts are available to serve different purposes. A trust may be *revocable*, meaning its terms may be amended, or it is *irrevocable*, in which case it cannot be changed or altered in any way. Consult with a professional advisor to determine if your estate plan can be enhanced by the creation of a trust. It takes time to create a trust and may require a sizable legal fee, although it often is less than the cost to your heirs of going through probate after your death.

Testamentary Trust

This type of trust is created in a will and takes effect upon the death of the person who funds it with estate assets. Like a revocable living trust, your assets can be distributed as you choose. This is less expensive to set up, being part of your will, but it can be much more expensive and time-consuming for your heirs after your death because it does not avoid probate.

Charitable Remainder Trust

This trust can be either in your will or in your living trust. It allows a person, while still alive, to leave a specified part of an estate to a favorite charity or nonprofit agency. The recipient pays the individual any income received from the investment, with reduced or eliminated state taxes, for the rest of his or her life. Then, on the person's death, the agency takes ownership of the investment. Another type of charitable remainder trust takes effect after the death of your heirs and saves only estate taxes.

Trusts and the durable power of attorney document should be reviewed and updated as necessary, along with your will, every five years or so. The documents, if not given to the person designated to handle your financial affairs, should be filed with your personal papers.

Community Property

In eight states, property acquired during the marriage is considered jointly owned. If one spouse dies, the property automatically goes to the survivor, even if only one spouse is listed as the owner.

Tenancies

If you and your partner, either married or unmarried, are considering buying a home together, you should decide how to hold this property.

Joint Tenants with Right of Survivorship

Shares held in an account are undivided and owned equally by the individuals whose names appear on the property (often spouses and/or children). Upon the death of one owner, ownership passes to the remaining asset owner(s). So if a husband and wife are joint tenants of a house, upon the death of one spouse, the property goes to the other. This transfer of assets avoids probate, but estate taxes will be due. A trust or will does not affect or control this equal distribution.

Tenants in Common

Here assets may be held by two or more people, who are the tenants in common (not necessarily owning equal shares). When one owner dies, as stipulated in the person's will, the deceased person's portion of the assets pass only to his or her heirs, such as children or grandchildren, rather than to the other tenant(s) in common (usually the spouse). Assets within the estate that are held by tenants in common *do not avoid* probate.

Tenancy by the Entirety

This agreement specifies that when property is owned together by a married couple, one spouse cannot terminate the other's rights except by divorce or consent. The assets of one spouse are protected from the creditors of the other spouse. This tenancy is only in effect in some states.

Provision for a Partner

You may provide in your will or trust that your partner can remain in a home you own until his or her death, after which the property passes to your heirs. You may also specify that this is in effect only if your partner actually continues to live in the home and does not remarry. (**Barbara**, who leaves her home to her daughter, gives **Leonard** the right to live in it until his death.)

Retirement Living Facilities

While many older couples continue to live in their own houses, condominiums, or rental apartments, the time may come when such independent living is no longer feasible. Some alternative must be found. The following are the kinds of senior retirement homes and communities commonly available.

Retirement Communities

Residences are purchased from a developer, an association, or a prior owner, and monthly dues pay for normal upkeep, repairs, and services. These communities range from private homes, senior apartments, and condominiums in gated communities to mobile-home parks. A minimum age usually is required for residency. While such a residence may be considered costly, the facility provides privacy along with extensive recreational and social activities. Usually a planned adult community does not directly offer medical care or meal services, although some offer private, on-call medical service or convenient transportation to such facilities. An inviting restaurant often is on the grounds. **Naomi** and **David**, **Edna** and **Seymour**, and **Nancy** and **Pat** live in such communities.

Congregate Living Facility

A step toward additional care can be to rent rather than purchase a residence. There may be a sizeable entrance fee for such a facility. This is usually an apartment where housekeeping services, group meals, and planned activities for residents are provided. Many facilities include transportation to nearby city shopping and medical services. Health qualifications for residents include being ambulatory (mobile and not confined to bed), while some provide a degree of "one-to-one" attention. Private, on-call medical care may be offered. **Mary** and **Fred**, and **Laura** and **Ed** live in such a residence.

Residential Facility

The next step toward more care is designed for individuals who are advanced in age or quite frail, but are still ambulatory. Such a facility usually is licensed and supervised by a state agency. It provides all the services of a congregate living facility as well as daily help such as monitoring medication, aid with bathing, and help with personal tasks. No onsite medical care is offered, but private care is on call. Monthly fees are appreciably higher than those for a congregate facility.

Long-Term-Care Facilities

As with retirement living facilities, there are different types of long-term-care facilities. The least costly is *custodial care*, which provides assisted services for persons with limited or no ambulatory ability for such things as getting out of bed, eating, bathing, and walking, but does not require qualified health professionals. A second level builds on custodial care and is *intermediate care* that may require a qualified nurse, but for limited purposes.

The most comprehensive and expensive program is *skilled nursing care* for life. It is usually prescribed by a medical doctor and provides services of qualified nurses on a 24-hour basis. There is an initial entrance cost and a monthly rental charge.

Often a contract is required, and applicants must demonstrate the ability to meet all financial requirements. Subsidized rates for individuals with limited or fixed retirement income, or qualification for Medicaid after assets are exhausted, may be acceptable. Also, most long-term-care facilities require an initial health examination, and admission is dependent on the results.

Convalescent clinic or hospital services are available to residents on a temporary basis during illness. If a resident becomes so ill as to be unable to function in the facility, he or she would be moved to a hospital or hospice care.

Long-Term-Care Insurance

Today the average nursing-home costs can reach as much as $60,000 a year. Therefore, extended nursing-home care or home health care can quickly wipe out an individual's or a family's financial assets. While governmental support for long-term-care is being considered by lawmakers, at present, each individual or family must make their own decision regarding the purchase of long-term-care insurance.

While such insurance can protect against the high cost of health care, it is not needed by everyone. If you can afford to pay for your own care, it may not be worth the premium expense. An exception might be if you want to protect your assets to pass them on to heirs or to charities. Individuals with few assets and low income usually qualify for governmental assistance through Medicaid. Persons with modest assets and average income are the ones most in need of long-term-care insurance. Many retirement plans and major insurance companies make this protection available.

If you decide that this insurance protection is important, generally you should consider buying it when you are between the ages of 55 and 63. For example, a premium might be about

$2,100 a year at age 63 while it is $5,500 at age 75 (costs are sub-ject to change). Carefully consider the terms of a policy, including its length (for your lifetime or for a set number of years), options for home care or nursing-home care, and other conditions or restrictions. Inflation protection can be beneficial if increases in cost are anticipated. Make sure the company is financially strong. Look for at least an AA rating from Standard & Poor's or Moody's rating services. (See the Weiss insurance company's rating web-site in references at end of the chapter.)

To protect their inheritance and peace of mind, some children are purchasing long-term-care policies for their parents. Children in their prime earning years may be more likely to have adequate cash flow to meet these costs than their asset-rich parents have when now living on limited fixed incomes.

Finally, a report in the *AARP Bulletin* (July–August 1999, page 7) and supported by articles in *Money* magazine and *U.S. News and World Report* magazine indicate that most Americans over age 65 live independently, with fewer than 5% in nursing homes, while those reaching the age of 85 eventually need long-term care. But consider the following facts, as they could influence your deci-sion about purchasing long-term-care insurance:

- Average nursing-home stay is $2\frac{1}{2}$ years
- 90% of patients stay less than four years in a long-term-care facility
- Only Alzheimer's patients tend to have longer-than-average stays

For professional help with the legal, financial, and related mat-ters treated in this chapter, contact an accountant, financial plan-ner, or lawyer who is familiar with the needs of senior citizens. In some communities, the services of a geriatric-care manager may be available. Also, check the references that follow.

References

AARP Publications (AARP Fulfillment, 601 E Street NW, Washington, DC 20049):

A Consumers Guide to Probate (stock no. 13822).

Getting Married After 50 (Investment Programs Financial Library).

Organizing Your Future: A Guide to Decision-Making in Your Later Years (stock no. D13877).

Product Report: Wills and Living Trusts (stock no. D14535).

Tomorrow's Choices: Preparing Now for Future Legal, Financial, and Health Care Decisions (stock no. D13479).

All New Avoiding the Medicaid Trap: How to Beat the Catastrophic Costs of Nursing Home Care, by Armond Budish; New York: Henry Holt and Co. (1995).

American Bar Association Legal Guide for Older Americans, American Bar Association Commission on Legal Problems for the Elderly, 7449 15th Street NW, Washington, DC 20005-1022.

The Elder Law: A Legal and Financial Guide to Later Life, by Peter J. Strauss and Nancy M. Lederman; New York: Facts on File, Inc. (1996).

Financial Fitness for Living Together, by Elizabeth Lewin; New York: Facts on File, Inc. (1996).

Financial Self-Defense for Unmarried Couples: How to Gain Financial Protection Denied by the Law, by Larry Elkin; New York: Doubleday (1994).

Leaving Money Wisely: Creative Estate Planning for Middle- and Upper-Income Americans, by David W. Belin; Old Tappin, NJ: Simon & Schuster (1993).

The Living Together Kit: A Legal Guide for Unmarried Couples, by Toni Ihara and Ralph Warner; Berkeley, CA: Nolo Press (1994).

Living Trusts and Simple Ways to Avoid Probate, by Karen Ann Rolcik; Naperville, IL: Sourcebooks (1998).

Love After 50: The Complete Legal and Financial Guide, by Johnette Duff and George Truitt; Orlando, FL: Love and Money Press (1994).

Plan Your Estate: Absolutely Everything You Need to Know to Protect Your Loved Ones, by Denise Clifford and Cora Jordan. Berkeley; CA: Nolo Press (1998).

Planning for Incapacity: A Self-Help Guide to Advance Directives, Legal Counsel for the Elderly, Inc., P.O. Box 96474, Washington, DC 20090.

Talking Money: Everything You Need to Know About Your Finances and Your Future, by Jean Chatsky, New York: Warner Books (2001).

Useful Websites

www. aarp.org (American Association of Retired Persons)

www.elderweb.com

www.longtermcareinsurance.org

www.ushc-online.org (United Seniors Health Cooperative)

www.nolo.com (Internet site at the Self-Help Law Center from Nolo Press; includes legal tips to help non-traditional families plan for the future)

www.weissratings.com

PART THREE:

How Do You Find a Partner?

CHAPTER 23

Are You Ready?

How Ready Are You for Commitment and Intimacy?

Being ready is as much within your heart as it is within your head. It is something you gradually come to recognize on both a head and heart level.

Many of us talk about wanting to meet someone of the opposite sex, a potential life partner, but we may not be emotionally prepared to start the search process. For others, their actions do not go beyond words because, on an unconscious level, something is holding them back. Others may rush too quickly into their search for a partner, which can lead to forming an unsatisfactory relationship.

Hasty Action

Rushing into a new relationship is usually a panic response that happens shortly after a divorce or the death of a spouse. In the initial anxiety to find someone to fill the newly painful gap in one's life, clues are often overlooked that would ordinarily keep one from making poor choices. For example, **Seymour** married quite soon after his wife's death. He only noticed the externals of his new wife. She was of his religion and was wealthy. However, he failed to see that she had a drinking problem, which was an enormous barrier between them. The marriage lasted only a few months.

Ralph lost his first wife to breast cancer after six years of marriage. Within six months, he married a woman 16 years younger than himself. In Ralph's own words, "This was a big mistake. She married me for my money. She disliked my kids and they hated her. It was stupid on my part." Ralph divorced her after only four months.

Bob, a good friend of my husband, Jerry, had an experience similar to those of Seymour and Ralph. After thirty-six years of marriage (with a sex life that was infrequent and of limited pleasure), his wife died. Bob found himself longing for love, companionship, and sexual fulfillment. About six months after his wife's death, he contacted a dating service. Through it he met a woman who was extremely attractive. He was completely blinded, swept off his feet, and they were married within a few months. It was doomed from the start. Bob was not happy living in her city apartment and she despised his country home and way of life. Her extravagant lifestyle and insistence that he pay all her expenses cost him a great deal financially. They had frequent, bitter arguments and marriage counseling was of no help. Bob left her and initiated a divorce three months after the marriage. He has since learned that friends and family who met her wondered how he could have picked someone with whom he was so poorly matched. Some had hinted their concern to him, but most were reluctant to say anything.

Bob, like Seymour and Ralph, reacted emotionally after his wife's death by quickly remarrying without ever asking himself the question: *Am I ready?* He just jumped into deep water, came to the surface just before drowning, and revived to an eventual good life. Fortunately, Bob was able to find happiness with another wife, but not before learning an important lesson the hard way.

Once the Grieving Is Over

Ralph, **Seymour**, and Bob were, in a way, fortunate. They were able to end their hasty marriages quickly. Others may still be living in unhappy marriages they made too soon after a painful loss. You need to be sure you are not merely running from grief, or from the fear of being alone, when seeking a new love after losing your mate. On the other hand, it is important to realize that if you have been with your partner through a long illness, a great deal of grieving has been done in advance. Then the death of a dear one can be almost a relief, and you may be ready for companionship, love, and sex much sooner than is conventionally thought to be proper.

This was true for **Stuart**. He had nursed his wife through seven long years of illness. Shortly after her death, he began to court **Donna**, and they married just ten months after his wife's death. This shocked some members of their conservative, religious community. But, according to Stuart, "I had a long, slow time to say goodbye to my wife. When God took her to Heaven, I knew He was right in taking her and that He has blessed my union with Donna."

If widowed, you need not feel disloyal in wanting to love someone other than your deceased mate. He or she would have wanted your future happiness. If divorced, it is good to trust that you can make a better choice and find fulfillment in a new partnership.

The Benefits of Independence

Contrary to the notion that you can't teach an old dog new tricks, we can continue to grow and develop as long as we live. **Karin** and **Naomi**, both widowed after long marriages in which they were primarily homemakers, gained self-confidence through employment and independent activities. The experiences of being independent and spreading their wings as older women, helped them to develop into more mature persons, and thus made them ready for satisfying new relationships.

Women Who Led Sheltered Lives

Women who were sheltered by their marriages may not be ready to be out in the world alone and may plunge into a relationship too soon after a death. Many older women are of a generation that traditionally did not work outside the home, nor did they have experience in handling finances or investments. Some went few places without their husbands. For such women, being alone can be quite frightening.

Several years ago, I led a small therapy group of widows, all quite advanced in years. Their husbands had handled all the family finances, and we spent quite a lot of time going over such practical matters as paying bills and balancing a checkbook. These women were even apprehensive about going places alone. To help them gain some confidence, I gave homework assignments, and if a member succeeded in going for a cup of coffee alone, and later perhaps attending a movie by herself, she received applause and congratulations from the group.

It can be a challenge to learn new and more independent ways of functioning. However, many older women find happiness when a new partner takes care of many of their needs and they continue to fulfill roles they have become comfortable with.

Men's Need for Close Ties

Many men do not have close friends with whom they can share intimate feelings, particularly grief. Many describe their wives as "my best friend." She may also have been the one who arranged their social lives and kept in touch with friends. When she dies, such a man can indeed feel lost. **David** was such a man. He had a very close tie with his first wife. He had male friends, but these friendships were based mainly on activities they did together, such as golfing and fishing. Usually these associations are not intimate and, as the men grow older, their activities and comradeships fade away, as they did in David's case. David met **Naomi** just a few months after his wife died. Fortunately, this rather rushed marriage has lasted thirteen years and has worked out well. David's wife is his one really intimate friend and through her they have an active social life.

Often if a man chooses out of urgent need, he does not choose wisely. An alternative would be to take some time to learn to make close friendships on his own. Then he might be in a better position to enter into a relationship where a new partner is not his only source of emotional support. **John** is an example of such a man. He has a number of close male friends and does not depend solely on **Karin** for his social network.

Help for the Bereaved and Divorced

After a death of a loved one, both men and women can get help through a grief support group (usually found through a hospital or a hospice service) or by individual counseling. Grief groups deal not only with the initial grief but also with how to get on with your life alone and perhaps eventually to find a new partner. Groups for survivors of divorce are also available through counseling agencies and private psychotherapists. Sometimes they are advertised in local newspapers.

Cliff was very depressed after his divorce. In addition to reading extensively about relationships, he decided to attend a support group. He said, "I learned a great deal about myself, my errors in choosing women, and how I could be different the next time around. At times it was painful, but it was certainly worth the time and money."

After a divorce or a long, unsatisfactory relationship, many say they want a new relationship, but because of painful experiences they are afraid and distrustful. They may go through the first steps of searching but never find anyone who pleases them. On a deeper level, such individuals are not ready for commitment. They are afraid to repeat the mistakes of the past and don't really trust themselves to choose a kinder, more loving partner. Because our parents are our first and primary role models for relationships, bad parenting can leave people unable to recognize a good potential partner. Indeed, many unsatisfactory relationships are a repetition of childhood traumas, and these painful experiences often lead to an avoidance of commitment.

Certainly there are many individuals who are perfectly content with being alone. It is the conflict between wanting intimacy and fear of it that provokes anxiety. For those who fear a close relationship because of early pain, personal therapy might be appropriate.

If you are bereaved after a long marriage, you may need the developmental experiences of meeting other people. For both the widowed and the divorced, contacting interest groups like those listed in the next chapter, *Locating Potential Partners: Sources for a Search*, can be an appropriate first step. Such groups can be very helpful to those who are newly single. They provide safe interactions with members of the opposite sex who are kind and decent people, helping to overcome the fear of forming new relationships. Young teenagers often form friendship groups of both sexes before dating and, surprisingly, the same principle may be true for you at this stage of your life.

Andy joined a singles group after his divorce, and the experience provided an excellent transition period for him. "After a bad marriage and a difficult divorce, I went through some pretty hard times," Andy said. "It wasn't easy to trust women again. The singles groups were fun. I met a lot of nice women and began to realize that women are human beings too. It made me ready for **Joanne**."

Happy to Be Single

This title describes what is true for many older individuals. Even I, happily married to Jerry, now and then enjoy a week or more to myself, doing exactly what I want to do, when I want to do it. For many, this freedom is hard to relinquish, especially if you've spent many years alone. My friend Alice, who has been divorced for many years and lives alone, cannot imagine sharing her home and time with a man.

I have met many women who, widowed or divorced, had for many years been controlled by their husbands. Now they very much enjoy making their own decisions and leading their own lives. They cannot imagine having this freedom in a new relationship and want no part of one. This can also be true of men who felt controlled by their wives.

Finally, many people do not want to risk experiencing the pain of divorce or bereavement again, and therefore prefer the safety of being single. Life can be full enough with friends, family, and interesting activities. It's fine to be happy while you're single, but remember, circumstances and your own feelings may change, and that's O.K. too.

Some Final Thoughts

It often takes time to be comfortable with your single-self before you are ready to become part of a couple again. In addition, it is important to know yourself to be truly ready for a new relationship. You may well ask, *"How do I know when I'm ready?"* First, don't be in a hurry soon after a loss from either death or divorce. At this difficult time, you might be desperately lonely and therefore not choose wisely. You might need time to grieve or to work through bitterness and pain. You may need help to resolve some internal conflicts between the need for closeness and the fear of it. Seek support and comfort, but be wary of making long-term commitments. Groups for both the widowed or divorced can provide support and help.

Healing time varies for each individual. Part of being ready is not only knowing yourself but also accepting yourself and your needs. Gradually, as you begin to feel more secure and after you have found satisfying friends and activities, you may begin to feel that something is missing. You might start being romantically attracted to other people, even finding yourself fantasizing about one of them, imagining a loving relationship. You might be feeling more and more sexual. These are all signs that you are becoming ready for a new relationship.

Feelings of loneliness are natural. Wanting someone to love and with whom to share your life is a normal and healthy desire. In the end, there is no set time after the dissolution of one relationship for the start of a new one. You, and you alone, can best judge when you are ready to start your search.

CHAPTER 24

Locating Potential Partners: Sources for a Search

Once you are motivated and ready to find a companion, you should develop a plan of action. First, become aware of the people, places, and services that could lead you to potential contacts. In this chapter, we suggest some sources that can be found in many communities or through communications media like newspapers or the Internet. A good place to start is with your own network of acquaintances.

Friends and Former Acquaintances

Your friends all want to see you fulfilled and happy. By describing your needs and interests to them, the potential is good for being introduced to someone whom you might find appealing. Another strategy is to attend high school or college reunions and, perhaps, to look up former acquaintances or sweethearts who may now be widowed or divorced.

Leonard and **Barbara** worked in the same profession years earlier. They had developed a friendship and were attracted to each other, but did not act upon it because of other commitments. After his wife's death, Leonard sought out Barbara. Their ease in being together and the chemistry between them had not changed. They are now in a successful marriage.

Be clear and specific with friends when indicating your interests and those desired in a potential partner (lifestyle, recreational pursuits, hobbies, religious preference, political views, and so forth). See suggestions in Chapter 25 that can help you define desired traits in a partner.

My husband Jerry and I met through friends. He described to them what he wanted in a woman, and they contacted a friend of mine who thought I was a match. She called me, and I gave her permission to give Jerry my name, address, and phone number. (See Jerry's letter on page 281.) And so it began.

You never know where you will meet the right person, and sometimes it takes a long time and a lot of "dinners with friends," and blind dates. It certainly can be worth the effort, and you might feel much safer with an acquaintance of a friend than with someone from a less personal source.

Long Lost Sweethearts

Many older folks are searching for and finding long lost sweethearts. Our friends John and Susan went steady when they were in high school and college. They had planned to marry, but Susan's mother disapproved of John, and so they broke up. Each married another person, had children, and then grandchildren, but eventually were divorced. A few years ago, John began to search for Susan. He finally found her through a college alumni directory that listed women by their maiden names. He was living in California, she in New York state. He phoned her, and it was as if they had never been apart. Despite the distance, they visited each other's homes and Susan now lives with John in his rural California home. It's a very different lifestyle for Susan, requiring many adjustments, and she misses the closeness to her children and grandchildren that she enjoyed in New York. Compensating for these changes is the joy of having found each other again, and their loving relationship.

You can look for a long lost sweetheart by contacting a school or college alumni office. Or try getting in touch with folks from your hometown who might know the person you are interested in. Here are some websites for tracing down an old flame: class-mates.com, alumni.net, gradfinder.com.

Senior Centers and Activity Groups

Almost every community has a senior center that offers a variety of activities, some of which may be of interest to you. Involvement in a senior center can lead to finding a group of compatible friends and possibly someone special for you. But the hope of meeting that special person through a senior center may be limited, particularly for women, because of the paucity of single, available men. Also, women usually remain healthy longer than do men, so those men at the center who are available may not be as active or as vibrant as the women.

Many communities provide social and recreational activities for seniors or that invite their participation. You can become involved in one or more activities that are enjoyable to you and find other people with similar interests. Service organizations such as the Kiwanis, Lions, and Rotarians, and recreational groups for card playing, hiking, bowling, dog training, and dancing are examples. Nature and environmental-interest groups, such as the Sierra Club and the Audubon Society, can provide interesting activities and potential friends. The Elderhostel organization for seniors (1-877-426-8056 and www.elderhostel.org) sponsors numerous travel and educational activities specifically for seniors. Check your local newspapers or inquire about these types of organizations at your local senior or information center.

Whether or not you find a partner, you will be enriching your life by engaging in what really pleases you. If you do find someone who suits you, you will have similar interests to share in your relationship. **John** and **Karin** met while ballroom dancing, and they still enjoy dancing together. **Bill** and **Joyce** met when hiking with a club and now hike together regularly.

Singles Groups

Gatherings provide opportunities for divorced or widowed people to meet on a regular basis and get to know each other well. Many interesting social and cultural activities can be enjoyed with singles groups, even if you do not meet a special person. The disadvantage, again unhappily for women, is that often there are many more women than men in singles groups.

After some years of being widowed, I joined a singles group that was available to graduates of the university that I had attended. It made my life much busier and more enjoyable. I attended parties, went to museums and concerts, and joined a book discussion group. As there were far more women than men in the group, I soon realized I would never meet a partner there, but I did make quite a few new women friends.

On a more hopeful note, **Cliff** joined a singles group where he learned a great deal about women and relationships. Then, as a final bonus, he met his wife-to-be, **Janice**, at one of the group's dances. It might be easier for men to find partners, but both men and women certainly can enjoy the social advantages of a singles group.

Church Groups

Churches and other religious organizations encourage members to participate in activities that can lead to forming friendships with those who have similar values. Church newsletters sometimes contain personal ads that provide a means of meeting other individuals of the same faith. This is especially important if religion is central to your life. Faith was important to many of the couples interviewed. For **Naomi** and **David**, meeting at their temple was crucial to their forming a relationship. While **Donna** and

Stuart did not meet in church, their seeing each other as good Christians made them acceptable partners to each other.

Becoming active in your church can enrich your life in many ways. It can be a source of emotional support and offer you a chance to help others. If you meet that special person, you also will be together in your beliefs and values.

Personal Ads

Although some people feel awkward when placing or answering an advertisement, this is becoming an increasingly acceptable practice. Look through the personal columns in your local newspaper to see if a particular ad interests you. Or you might decide to place your own ad. Don't be discouraged if you do not see many senior entries. **Ellen** and **Ralph** met this way.

For a newspaper announcement, you need to be brief and specific with a few lively words to describe yourself and the type of person you are seeking. The cost is usually minimal. To ensure privacy, an entry is given a mailbox address for writing or phoning. When you make a contact that seems appropriate, you should arrange to meet in a public place such as a coffee house. Be cautious until you feel safe and comfortable with the individual.

Of course you always run the risk of meeting some unacceptable individuals. But if you have a good, long phone conversation first, you can weed out some of them immediately. If you meet someone who is unsuitable, make the meeting brief. Don't give up and stay positive. With each encounter, you could have an interesting conversation and learn something, even if that particular person is not someone you would want to see again. You can always end your time together with "It was so nice meeting you—goodbye." Don't be afraid of hurting the other person's feelings. He or she has knowingly taken the same risk as you have. It is more cruel to promise another contact and then never follow through.

Dating Services

Look for advertisements in the personal section of your local newspaper, or in publications of some religious organizations. Some of these services can be quite expensive, so be sure to inquire about fees, the methods used to match people, and the potential for a person of your age and sex to find a partner.

Some dating services work on a direct, personal basis. You visit the service office, where you are interviewed to identify the qualities you desire in a partner. Then, from their files, after reading personal descriptions and seeing photographs, you select one or more individuals to contact. Also, data about you can be added to their records for potentially interested clients to examine.

Be very cautious about investing a large sum of money in an expensive dating service. A friend of mine, an attractive woman in her early sixties, paid $2,000 to such a service. The service had solicited her with a questionnaire that she completed and returned. Then they telephoned her many times, convincing her to go for an interview and to pay their fee. They promised her sixteen introductions, but she received only seven recommendations, none of whom had the qualifications she had clearly outlined in her questionnaire and interview. She was so irate that she tried to sue the service, but they had already declared bankruptcy. If you decide to invest your hopes in an expensive dating service, I suggest that you ask for and carefully check references.

A happier story about a dating service relates to another friend of mine, also an attractive, interesting woman in her sixties. She joined a dating service for a minimal fee of $50 and then received a listing of men with brief descriptions of each one. She made selections that interested her and paid a small fee to receive a profile of each man and how to contact him. She persisted for several years, met some interesting men, and now lives happily with the man of her choice!

Because the pool of available men is smaller for older women, you might consider a dating service that draws from a large geographical area. First, however, you need to ask yourself if you would be willing to relocate if you found the right man. I believe the chances of men finding women they like from a dating service are greater, but still be careful to investigate the service you choose.

The Internet

The Internet provides many opportunities to find information about dating services, and e-mail allows you to communicate with a person who may seem interesting. If you are not computer literate, ask a friend or a grandchild for guidance. Computer training is available in many senior centers and local education programs.

By browsing with Netscape or Microsoft Internet Explorer software, or by using a search engine such as AltaVista, Google, or Yahoo, you can find home pages for dating websites (for example, www.personals.yahoo.com). At the time of this writing, there are a number of websites for seniors:

- match.com (post a profile by writing essays and answering a multiple-choice questionnaire)

- matchmaker.com (respond to questions including desired locations and religious orientation)

- myprimetime.com (online dating and supporting suggestions with questions to consider; available online newsletter on relationships)

- saferdating.com (cautions for cyberlove gone awry, tips for spotting liars, and dangerous situations)

- seniorfriendfinder.com (answers questions, searches for someone in a number of different ethnic groups and religious affiliations)

- seniornet.com (65 and older, including seniorwomen.com and seniormen.com.)

- seniorscircle.com (generic matching service for those over 50)

- thirdage.com (dynamic site for those who are 45–64; provides dating service and much practical information)

Some websites allow you to call up a bulletin board service (Usenet News, for example), permitting you to post and respond to messages. Other sites provide chat groups so you can communicate with others of similar age and interests. Be aware that some sites charge a membership fee for their services.

Be careful when using the Internet not to exchange vital information such as your address or phone number, and do not make commitments until you have the opportunity to meet face-to-face in a public place and feel comfortable with the individual. The advice about phone calls and personal meetings under *Personal Ads* applies also to the Internet. Remember that someone can write wonderfully in an e-mail but not be the same at all in a personal encounter.

Evaluate the practicality of the sources available to you and the ones you believe will be the most useful. Then utilize the planning suggestions given in the next chapter to examine your own values and your expectations of a potential partner.

CHAPTER 25

What Do You Want in a Partner?

After establishing your desire and readiness to find a companion, and being prepared to approach sources, you should ask yourself the following questions.

- What is most important to me in life?
- What are my values, and what kind of lifestyle do I want to share with someone?
- What characteristics would I like in a partner?

The answers to these questions take careful thought and may come to you gradually, but they will form a framework to help you define your own values and the type of person you hope to find. When you do meet someone, discuss your common interests and aspirations, and what you can accept in the way of differences. Then the answers can be clarified and refined as the relationship develops.

First, let us examine certain qualities essential in any relationship. (Of course, the pronouns *he* and *she* are used interchangeably.)

Essential Qualities

Honesty and Reliability

Can you count on him? When he says he will do something, does he do it, and how promptly? A person with a passive-aggressive personality will promise to do a task he really doesn't want to do and then put it off indefinitely. It would be more honest to say "I don't want to." Is he there for you in good times and bad? If you choose to remain together for many years, do you feel certain that he will care for you as you age?

Before the death of their mates, **Laura**, **Ed** and their spouses were friends as couples. They were able to observe each other's thoughtful interactions with their partners. Each was there for their spouse through illness to the end of life. Ed, ten years older than Laura, is now 90 and in failing health. Laura faithfully takes care of him, as he in many ways cared for her through the course of their marriage.

Empathy

Does she have the ability to recognize and respond to your feelings? If your partner has this quality, you know you are really being listened to and understood. Can you tell her about what bothers you and does she listen without being defensive? Is she there for you when times get tough or you are depressed? *Research shows that knowing how a person reacts when a partner expresses sadness is the most valuable quality for a lasting relationship.*

Barbara was able to understand and show genuine compassion when **Leonard** expressed to her his grief after losing his wife. This quality of empathy was important to Leonard in connecting with Barbara, and remains so in their happy marriage.

Characteristics

There are a number of characteristics for you to consider before you start your search and as you become acquainted with potential partners. Some items might not be appropriate when you first meet, but can be explored as your relationship develops. They all can be based on your own personal preferences and lifestyle. They are a matter of choice and compromise between you and your potential partner.

What is Your Philosophy of Life and Your Value System?

By reading the interview chapters of this book, you found many people expressing the beliefs and values important to them, and how their partners share, understand, or disagree but respect each other's views. It is not necessary for a partner to share all your views, but respect for differences is important. Often, over time, by listening to each other, the differences in viewpoints can be reduced.

When **Janice** first met **Cliff**, she was impressed because they shared the same values about social issues. She, as a child psychologist, and he, as a health-care provider, were concerned about the care of children and both wanted help for families living in poverty.

Another positive fit in values was found by **Donna** and **Stuart**. Donna saw Stuart as a good, moral, upright Christian man who did not smoke or drink. They were both very devout Christians, and Donna joined Stuart's church.

Edna and **Seymour** are an example of a couple having different belief systems who were able to comfortably accept each other's differences. Edna believes in reincarnation and the importance of astrological signs. Seymour does not hold these beliefs, but is able to give Edna the respect of not trying to change her convictions. To Seymour, Judaism is very important. Edna has not converted to his faith but is active with him in temple activities.

Gayle was very articulate in a prayer to her Goddess in describing what she wanted in a partner: "A man who is open-minded, comfortable with my feminism and my beliefs in a different theological system than most people have. He doesn't have to believe as I do but be comfortable with my believing my way." **Jim** fit this description and they are living happily together.

What Physical Features Do You Find Desirable in a Partner?

Physical features are often the first characteristics we notice. **Andy** was caught by **Joanne's** walk, which he said "had a lively bounce." **David** liked **Naomi's** well-built body and her artistic manner of dressing. Naomi thought David "looked adorable in shorts." **Mary** thought that **Fred** was handsome and well-dressed. **Ed** saw **Laura** as beautiful and loved her smile.

Certainly you should consider what physical traits you find desirable, but making them the prime factor is a narrow and confining way of looking for a partner. When I met Jerry, I was neither impressed nor repelled by his looks. My friend who called me about him had inquired as to his appearance and told me he was "just so-so." Now that I've come to love him, I find him extremely attractive.

As you come to care for your partner, a greater physical attraction can develop. Remember, as we age, our appearances change. A number of the couples I interviewed showed me photos of themselves when they first met or were married. Some of them were smashingly good-looking but are no longer as attractive. Yet, they still love each other and find their mates physically appealing.

How Do You Both Match Up Intellectually and Socially?

When you first meet someone, it is not too difficult to know if that person is intellectually stimulating. Does he or she hold your interest when you talk, or do you find your mind wandering?

Does he or she talk *too* much, particularly about him or herself? The ability to listen to another person is important. And remember that the person you find intellectually stimulating may not necessarily have the same level of education as you do. **Barbara** says of **Leonard**, "He is less educated but more intelligent than any of my previous husbands."

A wide variety of experiences can make a prospective partner interesting to you. **Stuart** had traveled extensively and lived in many countries, which was fascinating to **Donna**.

Says **Gayle** of **Jim**, "He's very interesting to talk with. He has eclectic interests in many subjects, and he is very perceptive." And Jim says of Gayle, "It's fascinating to listen to her talk."

Consider how well the other person interacts with your family and friends. These aspects of social behaviors are important to the future of any developing relationship. **Gayle**, after meeting **Jim**, was pleased with how he interacted with her friends at a dinner gathering. Shortly after they met, **Ellen** took **Ralph** to visit her friends. If he had not fit in well, Ellen doubts if their relationship would have continued.

Intellectual and social compatibility are important qualities that will remain essential to a couple throughout life, so consider them carefully. These traits add variety and zest to a relationship.

What Housing Arrangements Would You Both Prefer?

Consider your preferred living style—city house, apartment, or condominium; rural or waterfront location; retirement community; or even major time spent traveling in a motor home. Usually a discussion of these preferences will occur further along in your relationship, when you are considering living together or marrying. An exception is **Ellen**, who in her newspaper ad specifically stated that she wanted a man who likes recreational-vehicle living. She and **Ralph** are now living and traveling in their motor home.

Of course, once you are involved, you will know where your partner lives and how attached he or she is to a residence. As your time together increases, it is usual to spend more time at one partner's home. This may be because it is larger, more comfortable, or more conveniently located.

This brings up the question of where to live once you marry or decide to live together. A number of the men interviewed were quite content to move into their partners' homes. **Leonard, Paul, Bill**, and **Jim** all left their city or suburban homes to happily reside in their partners' country residences. The change for these men gave them new interests and activities in their retirement. **Paul**, who was raised on a farm, thought **Ruth's** home was familiar and comfortable, yet he kept his large, suburban home for five years, which was located at a distance. Paul and Ruth visited there frequently. He finally sold it because, after five years, he was ready to say goodbye to the home in which he had raised his family.

Ed relocated to **Laura's** home because his house held such sad memories of his wife's death. **Mary** moved into **Fred's** larger and more elegant house after their marriage, although it was in an entirely different community, away from her family and friends. The transition was difficult for her, and they eventually moved back to her community, buying an apartment together in a retirement development. Similarly, **Edna** and **Seymour** started out in her home but eventually bought into a retirement community together. **Naomi** and **David** did the same.

Often a couple initially lives in one of their homes, but eventually they buy a new residence together. This can give a real sense of it now becoming *their* home. Also, as we age, retirement communities offer real advantages. (This topic is considered in Chapter 22.)

Then there are those who choose to live separately, as do **Nancy** and **Pat**, and **Carol** and **Ron**. The partners in each couple have the advantage of living close to each other, making it easy to have both separate and together time and space.

Jerry and I had no such advantage. I lived in a medium-sized city and he in the country, more than three hours' driving distance away. For the first nine months, we commuted back and forth. Mostly I visited him, spending a week at a time at his house. Because the distance was too great and we wanted to be together, after nine months I moved into Jerry's home. Before I met Jerry, I never dreamed I would leave the community where I had lived for more than thirty-five years. Jerry couldn't accept city living, so I knew it was I who would move. It helped me to have the attitude that the move would be a new adventure for me.

I am still in transition. At first I returned to my city home twice a month to meet with clients, then once a month, and now only once every few months. My practice has transferred entirely to our rural community. My daughter now lives in my home, so I can return there occasionally to visit friends and to enjoy the restaurants, shopping, and cultural activities the city has to offer. Periodically, Jerry spends short periods of time with me there.

Are You Neat Enough for Each Other?

No two individuals have the same degree of neatness. As you visit each other's homes, observe how your habits differ. How critical are you of the other's habits, and how do you respond to criticism? What accommodations can you make together? If you don't like the way he washes the dishes, it might be best to wash them yourself. He could then do another chore of his choosing, and a power struggle will have been avoided. The two of you can negotiate, but acceptance of each other's ways is of primary importance.

Bill had moved into **Joyce's** home. She finds him not neat enough and tries to persuade him to change his habits. He sees this as her trying to control him, and thus a power struggle ensues in their troubled relationship.

When I first saw Jerry's home, every surface was covered with books, magazines, and papers. We agreed that his desk could stay a mess, but he would clean all the other surfaces. My neglecting to turn off lights upset Jerry very much. I now do my best to switch off the lights when I leave a room. When I forget, Jerry turns them off without a lecture.

How Important to Each of You is Your Partner's Financial Situation and the Sharing of Expenses?

As with housing preferences, finances might not be discussed until later in your relationship, but it should not be too difficult to ascertain an individual's financial situation early on. You need to ask yourself, "How important is this issue?"

Before you actually live together or marry, it is important to discuss how expenses will be shared for the household, entertainment, and travel. Details of how the couples handle financial matters are described in Chapter 21. Also consider any need for a pre-marital agreement, wills, trusts, and other financial or legal matters. (See Chapter 22 for information about these subjects.)

What Attitudes Do You Both Have Regarding Each Other's Children and Grandchildren?

Getting along with each other's children, and their acceptance of you, are important to a successful relationship. To what degree would children accept a new partner? What are some ways to encourage and support positive interactions fairly early in your developing relationship? And how might you handle resentments or negative attitudes?

We treat this topic in Chapter 16, giving many examples from the couples interviewed. Often, after an initial shock, children frequently accept and support a parent's new arrangement. But whatever your children's reactions, your relationship with your partner should be your first consideration.

How Do You Each React to Age Differences and Health Conditions?

While you may meet someone close to your present age, there is also the likelihood that you might be attracted to someone of an appreciably different age—older or younger. It is important to realize that in a reasonable length of time, health problems and other symptoms of aging will occur and must be prepared for and accepted. In the interviews, you found many situations of wide age differences (ten years or more) and even the beginnings of necessary caretaking by one partner for the other.

With **Naomi** and **David**, and **Laura** and **Ed**, the women have begun to assume the role of caretakers for older men. Though **David** is only three years older than **Naomi**, his health and memory have begun to deteriorate. Naomi is a very active person and is open about her unhappiness with having to give up many of her interests to stay home with David. This unhappiness does not interfere with her love and concern for her husband. The reader needs to know that feelings of unhappiness about caretaking do not mean you love your partner less or that you do not do what is necessary. Groups are available that can provide encouragement and support for caretakers.

It is important to share information with each other about present health conditions and support that may eventually be necessary. Discuss the advisability of both of you taking blood tests for AIDS before becoming sexually involved. As of 1999, about 78,000 people, aged 50 and older, had developed AIDS, up from 17,000 a decade ago. (Reported by the Centers for Disease Control and Prevention, May 2000.)

Even people of the same age vary greatly in physical vitality and intellectual alertness. Therefore, look beyond age differences. **Gayle**, who is ten years older than **Jim**, is an extremely active and vibrant person who, when asked about their age difference, replies with a smile, "Yes, Jim's younger than I am, and therefore it's more difficult for him to keep up with me—right?"

Jerry is nine years older than I am, but walks so fast that I almost have to run to keep up with him. And you should see him climbing a ladder in our orchard!

What Are Each of Your Food Preferences and Nutritional Habits?

This issue is actually more important than it might seem. It either can lead to satisfaction and support or to conflict and disagreements. As a relationship develops, nutritional likes and dislikes and the need for special diets can become extremely important. Accepting change to reach a middle ground and exploring new ideas need open-minded consideration.

How Accepting are Each of You of the Other's Smoking and Drinking Habits?

Smoking is one habit that is obvious at the start of a relationship. Can you live with this habit? Even if you don't live together, you will be living with the habit. Perhaps your new friend would agree to smoke outside your home or not in your presence. Or will you decide that you can't accept smoking and the habit must be ended? If this cannot be done, the relationship is not for you.

A problem with alcohol is not so easy to detect, as many persons drink socially or in secret. How many drinks does your new friend imbibe at one sitting? A person with a drinking problem can develop a tolerance for alcohol and may not appear drunk.

How many times a day does he or she need a drink? Does he or she become anxious if no drink is available when desired?

Do not make the mistake of believing that you can change these habits in another. A person must be strongly motivated to quit either smoking or drinking. For a problem drinker, a local Alcoholics Anonymous is an excellent resource. If you continue in the relationship, Alanon (a group for those close to an alcoholic) can be helpful to you. There you can learn how to stop the behavior that enables continued drinking, and how not to let your partner's problem consume your life.

Seymour married a woman he hardly knew shortly after his wife's death. At first he did not recognize her drinking problem, but after a while it became evident and he divorced her after six months.

Neither **Jim** nor **Gayle** realized that she had a serious drinking problem. They began to drink heavily together until, while drunk, they were involved in serious car accident. The car was totaled and Jim was injured. It was then that Gayle entered counseling and attended Alcoholics Anonymous. They are both now completely clean and sober.

What Are Each of Your Interests for Recreational Activities?

Sharing activities such as exercise and sports, entertainment, travel, and hobbies can contribute to the development of a stronger relationship. Sometimes one partner is already involved in sports, such as golf or tennis, and the other learns to play in order to enjoy time together. If you met through an interest group, it is natural to continue this activity as a couple.

A central theme of this book is the balance between separateness and togetherness. Certainly it is a plus to have mutual interests, but a couple often needs time apart, especially during the retirement years, when work and children no longer provide separateness. Most of our couples have arranged their lives so they have both separate and together times. **Edna** and **Seymour** are good examples of this balance. They play bridge and golf together and volunteer at a shelter for the homeless. By herself, Edna is a potter and a gardener. Seymour, on his own, collects Indian arrowheads and plays a leadership role in his religious organization.

Do You Accept Each Other's Professional, Business, or Volunteer Activities?

Participating in ongoing and new enterprises offers both financial and intellectual benefits. You must decide whether to encourage and support such efforts by your partner. Often older people, wishing to remain active, serve as volunteers in their community. As long as such work does not excessively drain one's energy or detract from personal or family affairs, the participant can greatly benefit.

Volunteer or professional activities can help the balance of separateness and togetherness. In their small apartment in a retirement home, **Laura** and **Ed** are very much together, but Laura finds time alone by doing volunteer work as a tutor in a nearby elementary school. **Janice** practices part-time as a psychologist, while her husband **Cliff** volunteers in organizations serving their community. **Gayle** is active in many community organizations in addition to her work as a sculptor and a proprietor of an art gallery, while **Jim** works as a freelance editor. They work together on Gayle's projects, both providing ideas and Jim doing the final editing and computer work.

When you begin to be involved with someone, consider how that person reacts to your activities if you still work, even part-time, or serve as a volunteer. How do you respond to your partner's employment or volunteer service? Jealousy of the time spent in these involvements may indicate an insecure person and trouble ahead.

Can You Accept Your Partner's Friendship With a Former Spouse?

Because most older couples have adult children, they often do not have the frequent contact with a former spouse as when younger children are involved. However, there might still be a platonic friendship between your partner and a former wife or husband. Could you accept this without undue jealousy? **John** is still quite friendly with his former wife, the mother of his children, from whom he's been divorced for many years. **Karin**, who lives separately from John, accepts this friendship.

What Interest Do You Both Have for Keeping a Pet?

Possibly one or both of you already have a dog or cat. We know that an animal can be an important part of any household, but some people do not like the responsibility of the care involved, or they may be allergic to animals. On the other hand, there are pleasures in having an animal and health benefits can result from the companionship a pet provides. Realize, however, that arrangements for boarding are necessary when you are away from home for any length of time. **Joyce** has a cat, and **Bill** has brought his dog into her home. **Leonard** went to **Barbara's** home with a dog that happily plays with her dog and cat. **Stuart** objected to **Donna's** many pets. To compromise, she kept only one cat that Stuart learned to accept. When forming a new relationship, be clear with each other as to what is acceptable to each of you in terms of pets.

A Time for Action

Once you are clear in your mind about the type of person you desire, it may be time to take action. If you find someone of interest through a church or an activity group, you will have had a chance to get to know that person in a social context. When you are ready, you might ask him or her to join you for coffee, dinner, a movie, or whatever you both fancy.

If you have located a person whom you have not yet met, an initial contact may be made by mail, e-mail, or telephone. A letter should be general and not lengthy (two pages maximum), yet provide sufficient information about yourself to stimulate the other individual to respond. As an example, see the letter below that Jerry wrote to me:

Dear Edith,

I recently visited a friend and his wife, Bill and Joan Jackson, whom I have not seen for some time. During our conversation, I told him that my wife had passed away two years ago and that I was interested in sharing my life now with someone who has similar interests and has both emotional and intellectual needs that match mine. Last Friday, I received a phone call from Bill to tell me that his wife, Joan, had spoken to a friend, Lynn Martin, and your name was mentioned as someone who might be interested in meeting me. I decided to write you this letter as an introduction and then follow up with a phone call. You are welcome to give me a call when you receive this letter.

I am in my mid-70s, 5'9" tall, slender, and in good physical condition. I act much younger than my age, both physically and mentally. I had a grandmother who attained 103 years, and my mother was 98 at her passing, so I have the right genes!

I find hiking, swimming, and other outdoor activities to my liking. For the mind, I am a retired university professor and author of three textbooks. I continue to write and engage in some professional consultations. I am interested in good nutritional practices, listening to Big Bands and Broadway show music, national and world events, wholesome television entertainment, and have the desire to do some traveling with a companion.

I left my city residence earlier this year and have settled in a comfortable home in the peaceful, slow-going foothills. Although I like to visit the "big city" periodically, I prefer to live in this natural, non-stressful environment. Twice a week, I join a seniors' hiking group, and we explore wonderful places in the mountains and elsewhere. You should see the waterfalls this year!

I would like to share my interests with a lady who is happy in jeans, likes to grow and pick her own fresh vegetables and fruits, but periodically would dress up to spend time together in other activities.

Let's make contact and go from there. I'll wait a few days until I am sure you have received this letter.

Looking forward,

Jerry Kemp

A phone call, either as an initial contact or after your letter or e-mail, can give you a more personal sense of your possible partner. The voice and manner of speaking tell so much. Then, if you are still interested, you can suggest a brief meeting in person in a safe, public place. An hour together can give you a feeling for the person and how well you might match up. The time can be extended if the two of you are really hitting it off.

Develop a plan of action! You need to have a vision of how best to move toward your goal … *and good luck!*

Less than a month after our first meeting, I wrote this poem for Jerry:

Jerry, Jerry, I'm so merry
That I've met you.
How could anyone who knows you
Ere forget you.
Time will tell what comes of us,
But for now it's marvelous.

Concluding Thoughts

It has been a deeply enriching experience to interview the couples whose stories fill this book. Their joys and struggles confirm my own experiences with my husband, Jerry, mirroring the opening lines of my wedding vows:

I never thought that love would come to me so strongly, so late in life. I am indeed blessed.

Our bodies may age, our memories may slip a little, but our hearts remain the same. The capacity to love deeply and to be as sexually active as health allows do not change. In fact, with added maturity and the awareness that time is limited, each present moment is precious.

The Capacity to Grow and Change

The ability to learn and grow continues throughout life. Some of the couples interviewed had stable, happy childhoods and good, long first marriages. After a period of being widowed, they now experience successful later-life relationships. But others had difficult, sometimes horrendous childhoods and painful earlier marriages. Yet, in learning from these experiences, they are also able to form satisfying later unions.

One benefit of a new, older relationship is that it gives individuals the chance to find personal strengths not previously developed. A loving partnership provides a safe environment for the freedom to thrive. **Nancy**, in her partnership with **Pat**, found a more confident and sexual self not previously experienced. **Jim**, in his relationship with **Gayle**, enhanced his emotional side. With Jerry, I have learned to be more outgoing and to laugh and play. Jerry has become more openly affectionate and can more easily say "I love you." We have both become more accepting of each other's ways.

Respecting Each Other's Beings

Throughout our stories of older couples, there runs a common thread. In virtually every case of a solid partnership, there is a foundation of mutual acceptance and respect for the other person as he or she is. This means accepting the little quirks and rough edges another individual brings to a relationship. These are the foibles and irritations of life with someone else. Paradoxically, such acceptance provides the safety that makes possible natural, gradual change.

No one likes feeling coerced or criticized. Remember the parent or teacher who demanded changes from you? This triggered resentment, resistance, and anger. But a compassionate request can prompt a change that is freely given as a gift of caring. This process is particularly essential in older couples, when the habits, attitudes, and simple ways of doing things are well established in each person.

A long-term study by psychologists Robert Levenson and John Gottman confirms the importance of this acceptance. In research that spanned more than 20 years, they studied more than a thousand couples, trying to find what keeps them together and what drives them apart. They interviewed 50 couples who had been together for 50 years or more, many of whom were still happily married. When asked by a newspaper reporter what these couples were good at, Dr. Levenson replied, "They are terrific at listening to each other. They have respect for each other's way of being. They are not trying to change each other. And you see it both in the big things like accepting each other's personalities, their strengths and weaknesses, and in the little everyday details of living." (from *The East Bay Express*, July 9, 1999, page 9)

Differentiation from Your Partner

The older individuals I interviewed had developed their own individualities and were able to make compromises in their new relationships without losing their sense of self. They are, as David Schnarel says in his book *Passionate Marriage*, "differentiated." According to Schnarel, "Differentiation is your ability to maintain your sense of self when you are emotionally and/or physically close to others, especially as they become increasingly important to you." (David Schnarel, *Passionate Marriage*, New York: Henry Holt, 1997, page 56)

The fact that one can have an intimate relationship at the stage of life where one is "differentiated" is in itself remarkable and is, perhaps, the reason why these older relationships are so joyous.

Forming the *We* While Preserving the *I*

Judith Wallerstein, in her book *The Good Marriage*, speaks of forming a *we*. She sees a young couple as "putting together a shared vision of how they want to spend their lives together—constructing the psychological identity of the marriage as an entity in itself." (Judith Wallerstein, *The Good Marriage*, New York: Warner Books, 1995, page 62).

Individual autonomy and the togetherness of the *we* are not mutually exclusive. A person who is not fully individuated could fear being engulfed by an intimate relationship and see requests for compromise as controlling. The older adult who is differentiated and has a secure sense of self is not threatened by the many compromises needed to form this *we*. Still, for the older individual who has been alone for a long time or is not yet emotionally detached from a previous spouse, it may take some time to form the *we*. For example, **Bill** has had difficulty bonding with **Joyce**, as he still idealizes his late wife.

In every good relationship, there is a balance between the autonomy of the individuals involved and the togetherness that they gradually form. In older couplings, this task can be easier because the partners are already secure in their own sense of self, but it can also be difficult because each person has spent many years forming separate values, attitudes, and habits.

Comparing Mature Versus Young New Relationships

An important question is *"What factors differentiate a relationship formed in later life from one formed when one is young?"* First, there is the difference in developmental stages. In our twenties, identities are often not fully formed. When young persons live together, their psyches often tend to merge rather than to develop independently. In later years, each partner has a more fully formed sense of identity. Thus the older couple can relish each other's strong sense of self, but habits formed over many years can lead to problems and require much negotiation. Respect for individual differences is most important when an older couple forms a new relationship.

Another difference between younger and older couples is their stages of life. A younger couple is just starting a family and embarking upon their careers. The older couple is close to or in retirement. Children may be grown or ready to leave home. Without the pressure of work or child-raising, there is more time to enjoy each other. The flip side of this is that there can be too much time together, and there needs to be time for separate interests and activities. The new older couple is left to fully know each other without filling the roles of Mom and Dad or an occupation, leading to either possible problems or a stronger bond.

Financial issues can loom large. A young couple is usually just starting out financially, and often accumulates assets together. Frequently for older folks, each partner has his or her separate income and assets accumulated over many years. Often income and assets are kept separate. There are many different ways to share expenses and provide inheritance, and they need to be discussed.

Unlike a young couple who, hopefully, raise their children together, each partner of a newly formed older couple usually has children and grandchildren from previous relationships. Positive relations need to be formed with each other's children.

Often there are different residential locations. Partners may have established themselves over many years in different communities. Therefore, one partner may have to make the difficult decision to move with all that it involves, such as loss of close friends. One alternative would be for both partners to move together to a new community.

Realize that sooner or later one of you could become a caretaker for the other. This could be true in an early marriage, but that eventuality seems far off. For an older couple, that probability looms much closer. As you become involved, ask yourself "Do I care enough for this person to care for him or her as health deteriorates with age?" Also, with a young couple, the death of a loved one seems in the distant future. Death, and the grief it entails, looms larger in the consciousness of an older partnership.

For the mature couple, there is the gift of wisdom gained over the years and the awareness that life is short. Individuals can grow and change throughout life. We can learn from mistakes made in earlier relationships. Sadness and pain from the past and the awareness that life is short makes each present moment precious and can add greatly to the appreciation of your new older relationship.

The Bonding of Sexuality

All of our couples were active sexually in the early days of their relationship, no matter what age they were when they first became involved. For most, their first sexual encounter marked the start of their commitment to each other. Others waited until marriage before becoming sexual. Many have continued with sexual intercourse very late into life. Those couples whose medical problems interfere with intercourse still express their affection for each other physically, and for almost all those interviewed, some form of sexuality helps to maintain the strong tie between them.

Living Together First... Does It Make for a More Successful Older Marriage?

A number of our couples lived together for a period of time before marriage. Others married without previous cohabitation, believing that such an arrangement was contrary to their moral principles or the expectations of family, friends, and neighbors. Considering the age of these couples and the prevailing mores of the times when they were raised, this is understandable. The question is, does cohabiting before marriage make a more successful union?

Judith Wallerstein proposes that many young couples "play" at living together. For a good marriage, she states, "the path depends on the motivations that have brought the couple together, and whether they use the time together to build a relationship that can become a good marriage. If it begins as play, does it remain play or become serious? Does it allow them to learn about themselves and what they do or do not want?" (*The Good Marriage*, page 176)

I believe that the couples interviewed did not "play" at living together. Many years of life and the ups and downs of previous relationships have given them the wisdom to seriously use the time to work out difficulties. Those of our couples who chose to marry after living together see themselves as making a public declaration of their love and commitment. A number of our couples living together have no intention of ever marrying, although they see themselves committed to the relationship for life. This attitude is prevalent among many older couples. Because they do not plan to raise children, they see no reason for marriage. There are also important financial reasons for both marrying and not marrying (see page 236 in Chapter 22). And there are couples, such as **Nancy** and **Pat**, and **John** and **Karin**, who chose to live not only unmarried, but separately, yet still in a loving relationship.

If you embarking on a committed relationship, you need to make the important decision of whether you will live together before marriage, or indeed whether to marry at all, based upon your own and your partner's personal values.

The Ability to Love Again

When the first marriage was good and ended in the death of a spouse, those interviewed shed tears when they discussed the relationship with me. But a happy new relationship need in no way negate or diminish the cherished years of an earlier marriage. This is important for both partners in a new relationship to understand, as well as for the grown children of the earlier marriage.

When I spend time in the house where I raised my family, I still have dreams of my late husband. I recently reminisced with my adult daughter about those precious years when we were a young family. She is glad for Jerry and me and also is relieved to know that I have not thrown away the past.

Gabriel Garcia Márquez, in his novel *Love in the Time of Cholera*, beautifully describes the ability to love deeply:

"He saw no reason why Fermina Daza should not be a widow, prepared by life to accept him just as he was, without fantasies of guilt because of her dead husband, resolved to discover with him the other happiness of being happy twice, with one love for everyday use which would become, more and more, a miracle of being alive, and the other love that belonged to her alone, the love immunized by death against all contagion." (Gabriel Garcia Márquez, *Love in the Time of Cholera*, New York: Penguin Books, 1989, page 203)

If you have the capacity to love, that capacity does not die with your beloved. As many of our couples demonstrate, love can be reignited at any age.

The Ability to Find Love Missed in the Past

Many of our couples have found in their new relationship a love never before experienced. They may have had a marriage ending in divorce or endured an unsatisfactory marriage ending only with the partner's death.

Joanne and **Andy** each had long marriages, each ending in divorces, that were lacking in intimacy, affection, and sexuality. These difficult experiences have greatly increased their appreciation of their present happiness.

Laura was, for years, in a marriage with a husband who was emotionally distant and sexually unfaithful. She, like many women of her generation, had no financial ability to provide for herself and her children. She was taught not to expect much for herself and to stay in a marriage no matter what. Later in life, after her husband's death, she found in **Ed** a man who offered her fidelity, companionship, and love.

There are so many reasons why an early marriage may be unsatisfactory. Our present older generation received tremendous pressure to marry relatively young. I remember my mother worrying that I would be an "old maid" because I did not find a husband while I was in college. (If I had married my college sweetheart, it would have been a disaster! I was too unsure of myself then and too immature to make a wise choice.)

Other early marriages replicate difficult childhood experiences. A little girl may have longed for the love of an emotionally unavailable father. As a young woman, she may choose a husband with traits similar to her father's, trying in vain to find the love she missed as a child. Some individuals repeat this pattern over and over again, and have a series of failed relationships. But this is not inevitable. It takes courage, hope, and trust to heal from earlier wounds, but as so many of our couples prove, it is possible to choose wisely in later life and find the love missed in the past.

Does an Older Woman Stand a Chance?

Many women reading this book will say to themselves, "This is all very nice, but there are so many more older women than men that I don't stand a chance of finding a partner." Unfortunately, it is much more difficult for an older woman to become involved in a new relationship. Victoria Jaycox, author of *Single Again: A Guide for Women Starting Over*, states: "An informal estimate given to me by the demographer Martha Farnsworth Riche put the gap between the number of women who would want a marriage and the number of men they might want to marry at as much as ten or even twenty to one." Then she concludes, "After a certain age, finding someone great to marry is like winning the office pool." (Victoria Jaycox, *Single Again: A Guide for Women Starting Over*, New York: W.W. Norton, 1999, page 246)

Certainly, if an older woman wants a new relationship, she could do all that's suggested in Part Three of this book, *How Do You Find a Partner?* But she needs to also find fulfillment in her single life. And paradoxically, by accepting her single state, and being an active and interesting woman, she is much more likely to find a suitable partner.

Young-Old and Old-Old

Mary Pipher, in her recent book, *Another Country: Navigating the Emotional Terrain of Our Elders*, makes a distinction between *young-old* and *old-old* with these words:

"My own belief is that loss of health is what delineates the two stages of old age. Until people lose their health, they are in the young-old category. Until people are ill, many keep their old routines and add some new pleasurable ones. Even if they lose their spouses, they still can enjoy friends and family. Retired people travel, do volunteer work, pursue creative activities, and play cards or golf. However, poor health changes everything.

"In America, the young-old are mostly in their sixties and seventies. When health falls apart, generally in the mid-seventies or later, the young-old move into the old-old stage. Susan Sontag describes the difference between the two stages of old age this way: 'Everyone who is born holds dual citizenship, in the kingdom of the well and in the kingdom of the sick.'" (Mary Pipher, *Another Country: Navigating the Emotional Terrain of Our Elders*, New York: Riverhead, 1999, page 28)

Couples who start their relationship in the period of *young-old* need to be aware that if they both live long enough, they will eventually, with increasing medical problems, become *old-old*, with all the adjustments that entails. As Bette Davis, the late actress, said, "Old age isn't for sissies." Much loyalty and mutual support are needed in those difficult times.

Some Helpful Suggestions

What have we learned from the couples who so freely shared their lives, loves, and struggles? Here are some thoughts that may reinforce statements made earlier in these conclusions.

- First, it is never too late to be in love.

- There needs to be a certain amount of negotiation and change in an older couple's union, but it is essential to have a deep internal acceptance of your partner as he or she is.

- In every good, older relationship, there is a balance between togetherness and separateness, and this balance varies with each couple.

- Sexual satisfaction is possible throughout life. Age is no barrier.

- Your loving partnership is more important than any small issues that bother you. Conflict is inevitable in all relationships, but avoid blaming, calling names, and threatening to leave. Take a "time out" until you both are able to discuss issues calmly. Don't hold grudges.

- A sense of humor can make problems seem much smaller, and it helps keep a spark alive in an older relationship.

- Accept that your partner has had previous loves. It is good to be able to share freely your past lives with each other without undue jealousy.

- Your children and grandchildren may or may not accept your new partner. Keep in mind that the relationship with your mate needs to be primary.

- Early in the relationship, discuss your financial arrangements, particularly how expenses will be shared. In time, consider to whom each will leave his or her assets, the advisability of Power of Attorney for Health Care, long-term-care insurance, and alternatives for various types of retirement living (see Chapter 22).

- When forming a relationship later in life, one of you is likely to eventually become a caretaker. Feelings of resentment are normal. You need not blame yourself as long as your actions are kind and responsible.

- As you and your partner come closer to the end of life, know that you might experience the pain of a loss. Be aware that present joys are worth the pain. Knowing that life is short, live each moment with your loved one to its fullest.

I end this book by again quoting from Gabriel Garcia Márquez' book, *Love in the Time of Cholera*. Referring to Fermina Daza and her lover, Florentino Ariza, both very along in years, he states:

"For they had lived together long enough to know that love was always love, any time and any place, but it was more solid the closer it came to death." (page 345)

May all the couples interviewed experience such love and joy until the end of their lives together. Whether you are searching for a new relationship or already involved in an older relationship, may you find a love that grows stronger with each passing year.

Edith Ankersmit Kemp

Jerry's Thoughts

In many chapters, Edith has given you her professional analysis and thoughts about our relationship. May I make a few observations?

When we told friends we were writing a book together, they often questioned how our marriage survived this task! Yes, we have had differences and conflicts. But by cooperating, sharing ideas, and even arguing at times, we have become closer. It's a good feeling. As Shakespeare wrote:

I count myself in nothing else so happy
As in a soul remembering my good wife.

(King Richard II)

INDEX

The following topics relate to experiences of the interviewees along with information provided by the authors.